The Faith and Life
of
a Free Methodist

Editor, Compiler: Lloyd H. Knox

Free Methodist Publishing House
Light and Life Press
Winona Lake, Indiana 46590

Approved and commended by the Study Commission on Doctrine:
The bishops with George L. Ford, Lyle E. Williams, Lloyd H. Knox, and
Jack H. Mottweiler, secretary.

ISBN 0-89367-003-0

Part One   Faith and Life
            (From Words of the *Free Methodist Discipline* — 1974)

Part Two   Faith and Life
            (From Words of John Wesley)

Part Three Faith and Life
            (From Hymn Poems of Charles Wesley)

Together these present historical, current, and poetic profiles of a Free Methodist.

Use: To acquaint with the faith and life of a committed Free
        Methodist, not the institutional organization.
     To enrich the devotional life — read a section each day
        with thoughtfulness and prayer. Read a brief
        selection from each of the parts.

PART ONE

Faith and Life
(From Words of the *Free Methodist Discipline* – 1974)

The Free Methodist Church

INTRODUCTION: PURPOSE AND CHARACTER

The Free Methodist Church is best understood within the framework of the biblical concept of the church, the perspective provided by its historical heritage, and its commitment to the needs of man.

The Biblical Concept of the Church

It is clear from Scripture that the church is *of* God and *for* people. It is his creation. Christ is its head. The church is the people of God chosen for a purposeful partnership in accomplishing the will of God on earth. More than eighty metaphors, word pictures, relating to the church appear in the New Testament. Each portrays a more profound reality than does the picture it brings to mind. The pictures together make clear the nature and mission of the church. Paul speaks of the church as "body," "building," and "bride." The most inclusive and perhaps the most significant metaphor is "body of Christ." The redeemed are spoken of as "members of the body."

What is the profound truth that the many word pictures convey? God — Father, Son, and Holy Spirit — takes a redeemed people into partnership to share in his activities and to realize his purposes. The church is the organic, corporate instrument God has chosen to remake men and society. It has a mission of holy love. The church exists to produce Christlikeness in men and their institutions. Thus our mission may be described as participation with God in

1

bringing holiness and love to bear upon the sins, hurts, and needs of men. This description of our mission is both individual and social. It points to a social relationship of men to God and to each other described in Scripture as "the kingdom of God."

The metaphors of the New Testament are made emphatic by the greatest portrait of all — the Incarnation, God made flesh. The church, enlightened by the Incarnation, continues the teaching and the ministry of its Lord on earth.

When the church is acting under the headship of its Lord and the inspiration of the Holy Spirit, it continues the story begun in the Book of Acts. Many are its wonderful achievements since Century One, and many more may yet be realized in the unfolding drama of the acts of the Holy Spirit through redeemed men.

The New Testament reminds us that the church visible is not the church ideal. Because the church is a divine-human partnership, sharing not only in the holy love of its founder but in the blemishes of its humanity, it is ever in need of renewal. God takes the same risk with the church in redemption as he did when he granted men freedom in creation. Just as God, the Holy Spirit, used the hands of the Apostle Paul in "special miracles" so he can use his church today. The results will be the same — the Word of the Lord will grow mightily and will prevail (Acts 19:11 and 20).

Historical Heritage and Perspective

Free Methodists turn to the story of the church in the Book of Acts and the other New Testament writings as their primary heritage. They derive from this record their main source of direction and renewal, generation after generation. Men of God have wrestled with issues both old and new throughout the centuries just as they do now. The issues, decisions, and actions of the church in every age are important to us.

From the time of Acts, Free Methodists can sketch a line of

2

descent spelled out in large terms as follows: They trace their spiritual heritage through those men and women of deep personal piety who in all ages have shown that it is possible to maintain the glow of spiritual fervor in the midst of paganism, apostasy, and the corruption of the established church. They trace the development of the Free Methodist Church through a New Testament, Catholic, Anglican, Arminian, Wesleyan, and Methodist tradition. This means they identify with the mainstream of development of the Christian church. They are not a sect. They do not have roots in the Calvinistic traditions developing out of the many-faceted era of Reformation of the sixteenth century. Thus they demonstrate that one can remain in the mainstream of the Christian church and still maintain a spiritual emphasis, which is the very essence of Christianity.

Their Catholic-Anglican heritage is seen in their openness on baptismal forms, their refusal to demand a particular millennial view, their commitment to the Bible as the primary rule for faith and life, and their vision of personal piety and discipline.

Their Arminian heritage is seen in their affirmation of the love of God in Christ, which seeks to bring every man to himself but grants to every man the responsibility of accepting or rejecting that salvation. Since salvation is a matter of one's relationship to Jesus Christ, they affirm the security of all who continue in fellowship with and obedience to him rather than an unconditional, eternal security.

Their Wesleyan line of descent is discovered in their commitment to salvation by faith assured to believers by the direct witness of the Holy Spirit and their confidence in a God who is able to cleanse the hearts of men from sin here and now by faith, fill them with the Holy Spirit, and empower them for the fulfilling of God's purposes in the world. The Reverend John Wesley wrote: "In 1729 two young men in England, reading the Bible, saw they could not be saved without holiness, followed after it, and incited others so to do. In 1737 they saw, likewise, that men are justified before they

3

are sanctified; but still holiness was their object. God then thrust them out to raise a holy people."

Their Methodist parentage is seen in Free Methodist organization. They are organized with lines of responsibility connecting local, district, conference, and denominational levels. Their concern is for the total church, not just for the local congregation. Their Methodist parentage is also evident in their social sensitivity. Free Methodists in their earliest days recovered the social awareness which characterized the Wesleys. Their vigorous position and activities against the institution of slavery and the class distinction inherent in the rental of pews to the wealthy demonstrated true Methodism. Born at a time when representative government was being developed by free societies, lay representation in equal number to clergy was a further evidence of awareness of social and political concerns.

About 1858, in western New York, the Genesee Conference of the Methodist Episcopal Church excluded several preachers and many members from the church on various charges and allegations, but really for their adherence to the basic principles of Methodism, especially to the doctrine and experience of entire sanctification. Appeals made to the General Conference were denied. Those excluded could not join any other Methodist body, for there was none that agreed with them on the issues on which they were thrust out. Therefore the Free Methodist Church was organized by a convention of lay members and ministers which met at Pekin, Niagara County, New York, on August 23, 1860. The first General Conference met on the second Wednesday of October, 1862, at Saint Charles, Illinois.

By 1960, the Free Methodist Church of North America had extended its borders to include many countries other than the United States and Canada. In Japan, the church had developed to general conference stature, and other nations were making progress toward mature strength. An autonomous church of mission origin in Egypt united with the Free Methodist Church in the merger of the Holiness Movement

Church in Canada and the Free Methodist Church of North America in 1959. It seemed that the time had come to provide for the establishment of general conferences in addition to the North America General Conference. Therefore, in connection with plans for a World Fellowship of Free Methodist Churches, the General Conference of 1960 defined two national areas outside North America as general conferences, namely, Egypt and Japan.

The 1964 General Conference of the Free Methodist Church of North America adopted an enabling resolution and revised its constitution to provide for the organization of general conferences in other areas of the world. The purpose of the actions taken was to provide for the more speedy evangelization of the world and the extension of scriptural holiness and its fruits by cooperative ministries of mature Free Methodist churches in many lands.

In order to conserve the essential features of Free Methodism, the resolution provided that each general conference must adopt as a part of its *Discipline* or manual of law a section on the Purpose and Character of the Free Methodist Church and The Constitution of the Free Methodist Church, to be identical in all general conference manuals.

The Needs of Persons

Free Methodists are committed to the task of understanding the most important needs of persons, institutions, and varying cultures so that they may minister meaningfully and redemptively to them. In the high priestly prayer of Jesus Christ, he called upon believers to live in this world actively and intelligently in order that the world might be led both to "know" and to "believe."

Free Methodists are aware of the demonic forces in the world which debase men, pervert the good, and lead men and institutions to ruin. They attempt to help men by restoring personal meaning in a time of depersonalizing developments.

Free Methodists openly rebuke anything in law, persons,

or institutions which violates the dignity of persons created in the image of God. They are committed to taking advantage of opportunities where as individuals, local churches, conferences, and denomination they can minister healing and redemptive helpfulness in the world.

Distinctive Principles

Free Methodists seek to express the concept of the church of Jesus Christ, their historical perspective, and the needs of persons in specific principles and commitments.

Free Methodists today seek to continue the mission of first-century Christianity which was recovered by John Wesley and the early Methodists who declared they existed "to raise a holy people."

Free Methodists are a fellowship of Christians in earnest to get to heaven and committed to working in the world for the salvation of all men. They place their commitment to Christ and his church above all others. They keep themselves free from alliances which would compete for their highest loyalty and from all which would encumber and compromise their effective witness to the Trinitarian faith and man's dependence upon the grace of God. The Christian denies himself, takes up his cross daily, and follows Jesus. He conforms to all the will of God as made known in His Word, and believes the conditions of salvation are the same now as they were in the days of the apostles.

In doctrine, Free Methodists' beliefs are the standard beliefs of evangelical, Arminian Protestantism, with distinctive emphasis on the scriptural teaching of entire sanctification as held by John Wesley.

In experience, Free Methodists stress the reality of an inner cleansing and power that attests the doctrine of entire sanctification, both in the inward consciousness of the believer and in his outward life.

Their worship is characterized by simplicity and freedom of the Spirit, untrammeled by elaborate ritual.

Free Methodists maintain a life of daily devotion to Christ that springs from inward holiness and separates the Christian from the world, even while he lives in the world. They believe the best way to keep worldliness from invading the church is for the church to invade the world with redemptive purpose.

They practice a complete consecration of every power and possession to the service of God and man. They believe so strongly in the mission of the church that they are committed to responsible stewardship in finance. Therefore they do not need to resort to commercial efforts to support the cause of Christ.

Free Methodists sense a special obligation to preach the gospel to the poor. The provisions of the gospel are for all. The "glad tidings" must be proclaimed to every individual of the human race. God sends the true light to illuminate and melt every heart. To savage and civilized, bond and free, black and white, the ignorant and the learned, is freely offered the great salvation. Jesus set the example. Of his ministry it was reported, "The blind receive their sight, and the lame walk, the lepers are cleansed, and the deaf hear, the dead are raised up, and the poor have the gospel preached to them." This preaching to the poor was the crowning proof that he was the one who should come. In this respect the church must follow in the footsteps of Jesus.

Free Methodists are committed to the New Testament ideals of simplicity and modesty as a style of life. They wish to call attention, not to themselves, but to their Lord.

These distinctives of the Free Methodist Church from its origin are still living issues. In every era and every land these distinctives are the witnesses of the church, needing utterance clear and strong that they may be heard and heeded amidst the world's confusing and misleading voices.

The Constitution of
The Free Methodist Church

THE CONSTITUTION:
DOCTRINE AND MEMBERSHIP
Articles of Religion

GOD

I. The Holy Trinity

¶ **101.** We believe in the one living and true God, the maker and preserver of all things. And in the unity of this Godhead there are three persons: the Father, the Son, and the Holy Spirit. These three are one in eternity, deity, and purpose; everlasting, of infinite power, wisdom, and goodness.

II. The Father

¶ **102.** We believe the Father is the cause of all that exists whether of matter or spirit. He with the Son and the Holy Spirit made man to bear his image. By intention he relates to man as Father, thereby forever declaring his goodwill toward man. He is, according to the New Testament, the one who both seeks and receives penitent sinners.

III. The Son
His Incarnation

¶ **103.** We believe God was himself in Jesus Christ to reconcile man to God. Conceived by the Holy Spirit, born of the Virgin Mary, he joined together the deity of God and the humanity of man. Jesus of Nazareth was God in human flesh, truly God and truly man. He came to save us. For us the Son of God suffered, was crucified, dead and buried. He poured out his life as a blameless sacrifice for our sin and transgressions. We gratefully acknowledge that he is our Savior, the one perfect mediator between God and man.

His Resurrection and Exaltation

¶ **104.** We believe Jesus Christ is risen victorious from the dead. His resurrected body became more glorious, not hindered by ordinary human limitations. Thus he ascended into heaven. There he sits as our exalted Lord at the right hand of God the Father, where he intercedes for us until all his enemies shall be brought into complete subjection. He will return to judge all men. Every knee will bow and every tongue confess Jesus Christ is Lord, to the glory of God the Father.

IV. The Holy Spirit
His Person

¶ **105.** We believe the Holy Spirit is the third person of the Trinity. Proceeding from the Father and the Son, he is one with them, the eternal Godhead; equal in deity, majesty, and power. He is God effective in creation, in life, and in the church. The incarnation and ministry of Jesus Christ were accomplished by the Holy Spirit. He continues to reveal, interpret, and glorify the Son.

His Work in Salvation

¶ **106.** We believe the Holy Spirit is the administrator of the salvation planned by the Father and provided by the Son's death, resurrection, and ascension. He is the effective agent in our conviction, regeneration, sanctification, and glorification. He is our Lord's ever-present self, indwelling, assuring, and enabling the believer.

His Relation to the Church

¶ **107.** We believe the Holy Spirit is poured out upon the church by the Father and the Son. He is the church's life and witnessing power. He bestows the love of God and makes real the lordship of Jesus Christ in the believer so that both his gifts of words and service may achieve the common good and build and increase the church. In relation to the world he is the Spirit of truth, and his instrument is the Word of God.

THE SCRIPTURES

V. Sufficiency

¶ **108.** We believe the Holy Scriptures are God's record, uniquely inspired by the Holy Spirit. They have been without error faithfully recorded by holy men of God as moved by the Holy Spirit, and subsequently transmitted without corruption of any essential doctrine. They are the authoritative record of the revelation of God's acts in creation, in history, in our salvation, and especially in his Son, Jesus Christ.

We believe this written Word fully reveals the will of God concerning man in all things necessary to salvation and Christian living; so that whatever is not found therein, nor can be proved thereby, is not to be required of one as an article of faith or as necessary to salvation.

VI. Authority of the Old Testament

¶ **109.** We believe the Old Testament is not contrary to the New. Both Testaments bear witness to God's salvation in Christ; both speak of God's will for his people. The ancient laws for ceremonies and rites, and the civil precepts for the nation Israel are not necessarily binding on Christians today. But, on the example of Jesus we are obligated to obey the moral commandments of the Old Testament.

The books of the Old Testament are: Genesis, Exodus, Leviticus, Numbers, Deuteronomy, Joshua, Judges, Ruth, I Samuel, II Samuel, I Kings, II Kings, I Chronicles, II Chronicles, Ezra, Nehemiah, Esther, Job, Psalms, Proverbs, Ecclesiastes, The Song of Solomon, Isaiah, Jeremiah,

Lamentations, Ezekiel, Daniel, Hosea, Joel, Amos, Obadiah, Jonah, Micah, Nahum, Habakkuk, Zephaniah, Haggai, Zechariah, Malachi.

VII. New Testament

¶ **110.** We believe the New Testament fulfills and interprets the Old Testament. It is the record of the revelation of God in Jesus Christ and the Holy Spirit. It is God's final word regarding man, his sin, and his salvation, the world, and destiny.

The books of the New Testament are: Matthew, Mark, Luke, John, Acts, Romans, I Corinthians, II Corinthians, Galatians, Ephesians, Philippians, Colossians, I Thessalonians, II Thessalonians, I Timothy, II Timothy, Titus, Philemon, Hebrews, James, I Peter, II Peter, I John, II John, III John, Jude, Revelation.

MAN

VIII. A Free Moral Person

¶ **111.** We believe God created man in his own image, innocent, morally free and responsible to choose between good and evil, right and wrong. By the sin of Adam, man as the offspring of Adam is corrupted in his very nature so that from birth he is inclined to sin. He is unable by his own strength and work to restore himself in right relationship with God and to merit eternal salvation. God, the Omnipotent, provides all the resources of the Trinity to make it possible for man to respond to his grace through faith in Jesus Christ as Savior and Lord. By God's grace and help man is enabled to do good works with a free will.

IX. Law of Life and Love

¶ **112.** We believe God's law for all human life, personal and social, is expressed in two divine commands: Love the

Lord God with all your heart, and love your neighbor as yourself. These commands reveal what is best for man in his relationship with God, persons, and society. They set forth the principles of human duty in both individual and social action. They recognize God as the only Sovereign. All men as created by him and in his image have the same inherent rights regardless of sex, race, or color. Men should therefore give God absolute obedience in their individual, social, and political acts. They should strive to secure to everyone respect for his person, his rights, and his greatest happiness in the possession and exercise of the right within the moral law.

X. Good Works

¶ **113.** We believe good works are the fruit of faith in Jesus Christ, but works cannot save us from our sins nor from God's judgment. As expressions of Christian faith and love, our good works performed with reverence and humility are both acceptable and pleasing to God. However, good works do not earn God's grace.

SALVATION

XI. Christ's Sacrifice

¶ **114.** We believe Christ offered once and for all the one perfect sacrifice for the sins of the whole world. No other satisfaction for sin is necessary; none other can atone.

XII. The New Life in Christ

¶ **115.** We believe a new life and a right relationship with God are made possible through the redemptive acts of God in Jesus Christ. God, by his Spirit, acts to impart new life and put us into a relationship with himself as we repent and our faith responds to his grace. Justification, regeneration, and adoption speak significantly to entrance into and continuance in the new life.

Justification

¶ **116.** Justification is a legal term that emphasizes that by our new relationship in Jesus Christ we are in fact accounted righteous, being freed from both the guilt and the penalty of our sins.

Regeneration

¶ **117.** Regeneration is a biological term which illustrates that by our new relationship in Christ we do in fact have a new life and a new spiritual nature capable of faith, love, and obedience to Christ Jesus as Lord. The believer is born again. He is a new creation. The old life is past; a new life is begun.

Adoption

¶ **118.** Adoption is a filial term full of warmth, love, and acceptance. It denotes that by our new relationship in Christ we have become his wanted children freed from the mastery of both sin and Satan. The believer has the witness of the Spirit that he is a child of God.

XIII. Entire Sanctification

¶ **119.** We believe entire sanctification to be that work of the Holy Spirit, subsequent to regeneration, by which the fully consecrated believer, upon exercise of faith in the atoning blood of Christ, is cleansed in that moment from all inward sin and empowered for service. The resulting relationship is attested by the witness of the Holy Spirit and is maintained by faith and obedience. Entire sanctification enables the believer to love God with all his heart, soul, strength, and mind, and his neighbor as himself, and it prepares him for greater growth in grace.

XIV. Restoration

¶ **120.** We believe the Christian may be sustained in a growing relationship with Jesus as Savior and Lord. However, he may grieve the Holy Spirit in the relationships of life without returning to the dominion of sin. When he does, he must humbly accept the correction of the Holy Spirit, trust in the advocacy of Jesus, and mend his relationships.

The Christian can sin willfully and sever his relationship with Christ. Even so by repentance before God, forgiveness is granted and the relationship with Christ restored, for not every sin is the sin against the Holy Spirit and unpardonable. God's grace is sufficient for those who truly repent and, by his enabling, amend their lives. However, forgiveness does not give the believer liberty to sin and escape the consequences of sinning.

God has given responsibility and power to the church to restore a penitent believer through loving reproof, counsel, and acceptance.

THE CHURCH

XV. The Church

¶ 121. We believe the church is created by God; it is the people of God. Christ Jesus is its Lord and Head; the Holy Spirit is its life and power. It is both divine and human, heavenly and earthly, ideal and imperfect. It is an organism, not an unchanging institution. It exists to fulfill the purposes of God in Christ. It redemptively ministers to persons. Christ loved the church and gave himself for it that it should be holy and without blemish. The church is a fellowship of the redeemed and the redeeming, preaching the Word of God and administering the sacraments according to Christ's instruction. The Free Methodist Church purposes to be representative of what the church of Jesus Christ should be on earth. It therefore requires specific commitment regarding the faith and life of its members. In its requirements it seeks to honor Christ and obey the written Word of God.

XVI. The Language of Worship

¶ 122. We believe that according to the Word of God and

the custom of the early church, public worship and prayer and the administration of the sacraments should be in a language understood by the people. The Reformation applied this principle to provide for the use of the common language of the people. It is likewise clear that the Apostle Paul places the strongest emphasis upon rational and intelligible utterance in worship. We cannot endorse practices which plainly violate these scriptural principles.

XVII. The Holy Sacraments

¶ **123.** We believe water baptism and the Lord's Supper are the sacraments of the church commanded by Christ. They are means of grace through faith, tokens of our profession of Christian faith, and signs of God's gracious ministry toward us. By them, he works within us to quicken, strengthen, and confirm our faith.

Baptism

¶ **124.** We believe water baptism is a sacrament of the church, commanded by our Lord, signifying acceptance of the benefits of the atonement of Jesus Christ to be administered to believers, as declaration of their faith in Jesus Christ as Savior.

Baptism is a symbol of the new covenant of grace as circumcision was the symbol of the old covenant; and, since infants are recognized as being included in the atonement, we hold that they may be baptized upon the request of parents or guardians who shall give assurance for them of necessary Christian training. They shall be required to affirm the vow for themselves before being accepted into church membership.

The Lord's Supper

¶ **125.** We believe the Lord's Supper is a sacrament of our redemption by Christ's death. To those who rightly, worthily, and with faith receive it, the bread which we break is a partaking of the body of Christ; and likewise the cup of blessing is a partaking of the blood of Christ. The supper is also a sign of the love and unity that Christians have among themselves.

Christ, according to his promise, is really present in the sacrament. But his body is given, taken, and eaten only after a heavenly and spiritual manner. No change is effected in the element; the bread and wine are not literally the body and blood of Christ. Nor is the body and blood of Christ literally present with the elements. The elements are never to be considered objects of worship. The body of Christ is received and eaten in faith.

LAST THINGS

XVIII. The Kingdom of God

¶ 126. We believe that the kingdom of God is a prominent Bible theme providing the Christian with both his task and hope. Jesus announced its presence. The kingdom is realized now as God's reign is established in the hearts and lives of believers.

The church, by its prayers, example, and proclamation of the gospel, is the appointed and appropriate instrument of God in building his kingdom.

But the kingdom is also future and is related to the return of Christ when judgment will fall upon the present order. The enemies of Christ will be subdued; the reign of God will be established; a total cosmic renewal which is both material and moral shall occur; and the hope of the redeemed will be fully realized.

XIX. The Return of Christ

¶ 127. We believe the return of Christ is certain and may occur at any moment. It is not given us to know the hour. At his return he will fulfill all prophecies concerning his final triumph over all evil. The believer's response is joyous expectation, watchfulness, readiness, and diligence.

XX. Resurrection

¶ **128.**   We believe in the bodily resurrection from the dead of both the just and the unjust, they that have done good unto the resurrection of life; they that have done evil unto the resurrection of damnation. The resurrected body will be a spiritual body, but the person will be whole and identifiable. The resurrection of Christ is the guarantee of resurrection unto life to those who are in him.

XXI. Judgment

¶ **129.**   We believe God has appointed a day in which he will judge the world in righteousness in accordance with the gospel and men's deeds in this life.

XXII. Final Destiny

¶ **130.**   We believe the eternal destiny of man is determined by God's grace and man's response, not by arbitrary decrees of God. For those who trust him and obediently follow Jesus as Savior and Lord, there is a heaven of eternal glory and the blessedness of Christ's presence. But for the finally impenitent there is a hell of eternal suffering and of separation from God.

* * * * *

¶**131.**   The doctrines of the Free Methodist Church are based upon the Holy Scriptures and are derived from their total biblical context. The references below are appropriate passages related to the given articles. They are listed in their biblical sequence and are not intended to be exhaustive.

GOD

I. *Holy Trinity*
   Genesis 1:1-2; Exodus 3:13-15; Deuteronomy 6:4; Matthew 28:19; John 1:1-3; 5:19-23; 8:58; 14:9-11; 15:26; 16:13-15; II Corinthians 13:14.

II. *Father*
Genesis 1:26-27; Psalm 103:13-14; Isaiah 40:28-29; 64:8; Matthew 6:8; 18:14; Luke 15:11-32; John 4:23; I John 1:3.

III. *Son — His Incarnation*
Matthew 1:21; 20:28; 26:27-28; Luke 1:35; 19:10; John 1:1, 10, 14; II Corinthians 5:18-19; Philippians 2:5-8; Hebrews 2:17; 9:14-15.
Son — His Resurrection and Exaltation
Matthew 25:31-32; Luke 24:1-7; 24:39; John 20:19; Acts 1:9-11; 2:24; Romans 8:33-34; II Corinthians 5:10; Philippians 2:9-11; Hebrews 1:1-4.

IV. *Holy Spirit — His Person*
Matthew 28:19; John 4:24; 14:16-17, 26; 15:26; 16:13-15.
Holy Spirit — His Work in Salvation
John 16:7-8; Acts 15:8-9; Romans 8:9, 14-16; I Corinthians 3:16; II Corinthians 3:17-18; Galatians 4:6.
Holy Spirit — His Relation to the Church
Acts 5:3-4; Romans 8:14; I Corinthians 12:4-7; II Peter 1:21.

THE SCRIPTURES

V. *Sufficiency*
Deuteronomy 4:2; 28:9; Psalm 19:7-11; John 14:26; 17:17; Romans 15:4; II Timothy 3:14-17; Hebrews 4:12; James 1:21.

VI. *Authority of the Old Testament*
Matthew 5:17-18; Luke 10:25-28; John 5:39, 46-47; Acts 10:43; Galatians 5:3-4; I Peter 1:10-12.

VII. *New Testament*
Matthew 24:35; Mark 8:38; John 14:24; Hebrews 2:1-4; II Peter 1:16-21; I John 2:2-6; Revelation 21:5; 22:19.

MAN

VIII. *Man: A Free Moral Person*
Genesis 1:27; Psalm 51:5; 130:3; Romans 5:17-19; Ephesians 2:8-10.

IX. *Law of Life and Love*
Matthew 22:35-40; John 15:17; Galatians 3:28; I John 4:19-21.

X. *Good Works*
Matthew 5:16; 7:16-20; Romans 3:27-28; Ephesians 2:10; II Timothy 1:8-9; Titus 3:5.

SALVATION

XI. *Christ's Sacrifice*
Luke 24:46-48; John 3:16; Acts 4:12; Romans 5:8-11; Galatians 2:16; 3:2-3; Ephesians 1:7-8; 2:13; Hebrews 9:11-14, 25-26; 10:8-14.

XII. *The New Life in Christ*
John 1:12-13; 3:3-8; Acts 13:38-39; Romans 8:15-17; Ephesians 2:8-9; Colossians 3:9-10.
Justification
Psalm 32:1-2; Acts 10:43; Romans 3:21-26, 28; 4:2-5; 5:8-9; I Corinthians 6:11; Philippians 3:9.
Regeneration
Ezekiel 36:26-27; John 5:24; Romans 6:4; II Corinthians 5:17; Ephesians 4:22-24; Colossians 3:9-10; Titus 3:4-5; I Peter 1:23.
Adoption
Romans 8:15-17; Galatians 4:4-7; Ephesians 1:5-6; I John 3:1-3.

XIII. *Entire Sanctification*
Leviticus 20:7-8; John 14:16-17; 17:19; Acts 1:8; 2:4; 15:8-9; Romans 5:3-5; 8:12-17; 12:1-2; I Corinthians 6:11; 12:4-11; Galatians 5:22-25; Ephesians 4:22-24; I Thessalonians 4:7; 5:23-24; II Thessalonians 2:13; Hebrews 10:14.

XIV. *Restoration*
Matthew 12:31-32; 18:21-22; Romans 6:1-2; Galatians
6:1; I John 1:9; 2:1-2; 5:16-17; Revelation 2:5;
3:19-20.

THE CHURCH

XV. *The Church*
Matthew 16:15-18; 18:17; Acts 2:41-47; 9:31; 12:5;
14:23-26; 15:22; 20:28; I Corinthians 1:2; 11:23;
12:28; 16:1; Ephesians 1:22-23; 2:19-22; 3:9-10;
5:22-23; Colossians 1:18; I Timothy 3:14-15.

XVI. *The Language of Worship*
Nehemiah 8:5, 6, 8; Matthew 6:7; I Corinthians 14:6-9;
II Corinthians 14:23-25.

XVII. *The Holy Sacraments*
Matthew 26:26-29; 28:19; Acts 22:16; Romans 4:11;
I Corinthians 10:16-17; 11:23-26; Galatians 3:27.
Baptism
Acts 2:38, 41; 8:12-17; 9:18; 16:33; 18:8; 19:5; John
3:5; I Corinthians 12:13; Galatians 3:27-29; Colossians
2:11-12; Titus 3:5.
The Lord's Supper
Mark 14:22-24; John 6:53-58; Acts 2:46; I Corinthians
5:7-8; 10:16; 11:20, 23-29.

LAST THINGS

XVIII. *The Kingdom of God*
Matthew 6:10, 19-20; 24:14; Acts 1:8; Romans
8:19-23; I Corinthians 15:20-25; Philippians 2:9-10;
I Thessalonians 4:15-17; II Thessalonians 1:5-12;
II Peter 3:3-10; Revelation 14:6; 21:3-8; 22:1-5, 17.

XIX. *The Return of Christ*
Matthew 24:1-51; 26:64; Mark 13:26-27; Luke
17:26-37; John 14:1-3; Acts 1:9-11; I Thessalonians

4:13-18; Titus 2:11-14; Hebrews 9:27-28; Revelation
1:7; 19:11-16; 22:6-7, 12, 20.
XX. *Resurrection*
John 5:28-29; I Corinthians 15:20, 51-57; II Corinthians
4:13-14.
XXI. *Judgment*
Matthew 25:31-46; Luke 11:31-32; Acts 10:42; 17:31;
Romans 2:15-16; 14:10-11; II Corinthians 5:6-10;
Hebrews 9:27-28; 10:26-31; II Peter 3:7.
XXII. *Destiny*
Mark 9:42-48; John 14:3; Hebrews 2:1-3; Revelation
20:11-15; 21:22-27.

MEMBERSHIP AND COVENANT

REQUIREMENTS, RIGHTS, AND TENURE

¶ **150.** The privileges and requirements of full membership in the church are constitutional, and changes therein may
be made only by amendment according to Paragraphs
225-228. Nothing shall be included in the membership ritual
that is contrary to the following definitions of conditions and
privileges of membership.

¶ **151.** The requirements of full membership are:

1. Christian baptism, confession of a personal experience
in regeneration, and a pledge to seek diligently until sanctified
wholly if that experience has not been attained.

2. Acceptance of the Articles of Religion, guidance for
Christian living [the Covenant], and the authority of the
Discipline in matters of church government.*

3. A covenant to support the church, to live in fellowship
with the members thereof, and to seek God's glory in all
things.

4. Recommendation to membership by the official board
of the church, the candidate's public declaration of member-

21

ship vows, and the approving vote of three-fourths of the members of the receiving society who are present and voting.

¶ **152.** The rights of full membership are:

1. Participation in the sacraments and ordinances of the church.

2. To vote and hold office upon reaching the age designated by the General Conference.

3. Trial and appeal if charged with failure to maintain the conditions of membership, with the specific provision that joining another religious denomination or sect shall of itself sever membership in the church without trial.

¶ **153.** Church membership may be terminated only by:

1. Voluntary withdrawal (including permission to withdraw under complaint).

2. Joining another religious denomination or sect or a secret order.

3. Expulsion after proper summary proceeding, or trial and conviction.

4. Persistent neglect of church relationship by a member residing at a distance from pastoral and church supervision, which in effect is voluntary withdrawal.

---

* When not in conflict with local laws in matters of church government.

COVENANT

Privilege and Responsibility

¶ **154.** Membership in the church is a high privilege and responsibility. We believe the covenant required of members is consistent with the teaching of the written Word of God. Faithfulness to the covenant is evidence of the individual member's desire to sustain a saving relationship with Jesus Christ as Lord, to bring glory to God, to advance the cause of God on earth, to preserve the unity of the body of Christ, and to cherish the fellowship of the Free Methodist Church.

¶ **155.** When a member does not keep his covenant and habitually violates his vows, it is the responsibility of minister and members to point to the failure and to seek in love to restore the member. If, after these steps have been taken, the member does not keep his commitments, he must be dealt with in accord with the due processes of the church.

¶ **156.** A member of the Free Methodist Church, trusting in the enablement of the Holy Spirit and seeking the support of the other members of the church, makes the following confession and commitments as a covenant with the Lord and the church.

The Confession and Commitment

I confess Jesus Christ as my personal Savior and Lord and will continue to walk with him by faith. I commit myself to know God in his full sanctifying grace.

As Regards God

¶ **157.** 1. I will reverence the name of God.

2. I will observe the Lord's Day in worship, Christian fellowship and service, renewal of mind and spirit, avoiding all unnecessary commerce, labors, travel, and pleasures which detract from the moral and spiritual purposes of the day.

3. I will not engage in any form of false worship such as spiritism, witchcraft, and astrology.

4. I will abstain from membership in secret societies and oath-bound lodges, and, recognizing that the religious nature of such organizations tends to divide the Christian's loyalty and confuse his Christian faith, I will keep myself free to follow the will of God in all things.

5. I will seek to grow in the knowledge and love of God by consistent use of the means of grace such as public worship of God, the ministry of the Word, the Supper of the Lord, family and private prayer, searching the Scriptures, and fasting and abstinence.

As Regards Myself and All Men

¶ **158.** 1. I will show goodness and mercy to all men, and especially to the household of faith, both to their physical and spiritual needs as I have ability.

2. I will respect the rights of all persons as created in the image of God, regardless of differences of sex, race, or color.

3. I will be just in all transactions, faithful in commitments and contract obligations with full intention to keep them.

4. I will abstain from the manufacture, sale, and use of alcoholic beverages and harmful drugs and from the cultivation, manufacture, sale, and use of tobacco.

5. I will abstain from all forms of gambling.

6. I will observe the scriptural standards of simplicity, humility, modesty, propriety, purity, and good stewardship in everything I buy, use, or wear, and hereby reflect the beauty of the gospel.

As Regards the Institutions of God

¶ **159.** 1. I will respect duly constituted authority in the home, church, and state except when it is in violation of the clear teachings of the Scripture.

2. I will observe the teachings of the Scripture regarding the sanctity of the home and marriage and the nurture of children in the Christian faith.

3. I will be guided by the teaching of Scripture regarding separation, divorce, and remarriage as understood by the church, especially recognizing monogamy as God's plan for marriage.

As Regards the Church

¶ **160.** 1. I have received Christian baptism.

2. I accept the Articles of Religion and the authority of the *Discipline* in matters of church government.

3. I will work for the advancement of God's kingdom and the mutual growth of fellow believers toward full stature in Christ in holiness and love.

4. I will seek to preserve the unity and the witness of the church by nurturing and expressing Christlike love as described in I Corinthians, chapter thirteen.

5. I will cooperate in developing the Christian fellowship by willingness to receive and give counsel with tenderness and meekness; to pray for others; to aid others in sickness and distress; to cultivate Christian sympathy; and to show understanding, courtesy, and purity in all conversation.

6. I will exercise responsible Christian stewardship by the careful and disciplined use of time, talents, and material resources, being sensitive to the needs of the church and my fellowmen. I will accept the biblical principle of tithes and offerings as the guide of my material stewardship and the support of the church. I will choose those activities which contribute to the spiritual, moral, intellectual, and physical well-being of myself and those who share in them.

THE CHRISTIAN LIFE

CHRISTIAN EXPERIENCE

PREFACE

¶ **300.** The Christian life can be consciously experienced because it is a relationship between persons — the personal God and humans made in his likeness. Every person is confronted by this personal God, and the outcome of this confrontation is primarily affected by how the person responds.

In love God has fully provided for the salvation of all mankind. But only those who respond in repentance and faith can experience his grace as a redemptive reality.

God deals with all men as free and responsible persons. Therefore, he not only makes his grace available on condition of man's free response, but he also reveals himself and makes known his life to all who put their trust in him. The redemptive relationship with Jesus Christ is experienced as an awareness of his love and fellowship.

Those who are justified by faith experience the peace of God. When his Holy Spirit comes to the heart, there is joy. The Holy Spirit's indwelling presence is the assurance of our relationship to God as his dear children.

AWAKENING TO GOD

¶301. The Scriptures teach that man is corrupt in every aspect of his nature and has gone far from original righteousness. Added to the depravity common to man because of the Fall there are the enslaving effects of committed sins. Man is unable in himself to come to God, but God in his grace reaches out to every sinner.

God takes the initiative in making sinners aware of their needs, using his Word, the revelation in Jesus Christ, the gospel proclamation of the church, the witness of individuals, and the circumstances of life. By such means, the Holy Spirit awakens sinners to their needs and to the truth of the gospel (John 16:8, 13). Awakened, they must make a response, either rejecting the call of God or turning to God in repentance and faith.

REPENTANCE AND RESTITUTION

¶302. Awakened by the Holy Spirit to his lost condition before God, a person may move toward God. Since "all have sinned and fall short of the glory of God" (Romans 3:23), all must repent in order to come into a right relationship with God.

Repentance calls for a sincere and thorough change of mind. To repent is to turn from sin with genuine sorrow and to turn to God in confession and submission. The whole person is involved: mind, feelings. will. Repentance is more than regret for wrongdoing or sorrow at being caught. It is personal sorrow that one has sinned against God. Repentance demands a radical turning from sin and a sincere turning to God. The result is a saving relationship with Christ.

Sincere repentance leads to moral renewal, often evidenced by restitution — the effort to right one's wrongs whenever possible. Acts of restitution, as in the case of Zaccheus, are certainly fruits befitting repentance (Luke 19:8; 3:8). Neither repentance nor restitution save, however, without faith in Christ (Romans 5:1).

CONSECRATION

¶ **303.** God calls his people to set themselves apart to his will and purpose (Romans 6:13; 12:1). Anything thus set apart is said to be consecrated.

All Christians are called to be holy and without blame before God in love (Ephesians 5:27). Christ demands that his disciples follow him in mind and spirit (Romans 7:24-25). If Christians are to witness effectively in the world, they must be distinguished by righteousness, peace, joy, faith, hope, and love (John 13:35; 14:15; Galatians 5:22-24). God wants a special kind of people for his work (Matthew 16:24; Romans 14:17; 8:6-9; John 17:17; Psalm 100:2). When a Christian sincerely follows Christ and listens to the Holy Spirit as he speaks in the Scriptures, he should sense his need of cleansing from inward sin. He should desire earnestly to be filled with the love of God and long for a relationship with Christ which will satisfy his deepest inward need and empower him to serve and obey his Lord (Ephesians 5:1-2; 1:4; I Corinthians 13:13; 14:1; Acts 1:8).

The Christian, therefore, must consecrate himself to God and surrender his will to the will of the Heavenly Father (Matthew 19:21). He who desires inward sanctification must deny himself, bear the cross, and follow Christ. Devotion to self is idolatry. A Christian who is divided in his loyalty cannot serve God victoriously and steadfastly. Christ must be given the preeminence. He must be the Lord of the Christian's life.

Therefore, to open himself to the sanctifying work of the Holy Spirit, the believer must give himself without reservation to God. He must freely yield all he has to the purposes of God and devote every desire and ambition to the service of Christ rather than to self (Colossians 3:8-13). No Christian can be delivered from the dominion of sin if he permits self to reign in his life. He cannot serve two masters (Matthew 6:24).

ENTIRE SANCTIFICATION

¶ **304**. Christ gave himself even unto death for the cleansing of his church (Ephesians 2:14-21; Galatians 2:20; John 7:37; Ephesians 5:25-27; Acts 1:8; II Corinthians 6:2). His disciples are called to be holy. Christ has provided in the atonement for the believer to be entirely sanctified. Sanctification begins with regeneration and results in a deeper relationship when the believer is fully cleansed in heart (Psalm 107:9). This cleansing accompanies the fullness of the Holy Spirit. Paul prayed: "May the God of peace himself sanctify you wholly; and may your spirit and soul and body be kept sound and blameless at the coming of our Lord Jesus Christ. He who calls you is faithful, and he will do it" (I Thessalonians 5:23-24).

God the Holy Spirit is the sanctifier. Coming into the life at conversion, he fills with his presence when the Christian's consecration is complete, cleansing the heart and empowering for witness and service (Acts 1:8; 15:6-9). He sheds God's love throughout the heart and life of the Christian (Romans 5:5).

Accepting the promise of God by faith, he will enter into a deepened relationship with Christ. He will be enabled to love God with all his heart, soul, strength, and mind, and his neighbor as himself (Matthew 22:37-40). He will know an inner surrender to all the will of God, and his life will be transformed from one of inward conflict to one of glad obedience.

Inward sanctification cleanses the Christian from sin and

delivers from the idolatry of self. When he is cleansed he is made perfect, not in performance, but in love.

THE GIFTS OF THE SPIRIT

¶305. The Holy Spirit distributes, as he wills, gifts of speech and service devoted to the common good and the building of the church. Gifts are to be exercised under the lordship of Christ. The believer is to seek as the evidence of the Holy Spirit's fullness, not the gift themselves, but the Giver. The greater gifts, however, are to be desired above the lesser. "Make love your aim, and earnestly desire the spiritual gifts, especially that you may prophesy" (I Corinthians 14:1).

The Apostle Paul gives guidelines, helping the church to discern the authenticity of gifts of the Spirit. The Holy Spirit brings order out of chaos. This is true of his work in creation as well as in redemption. He is never the author of confusion but is the source of love, power, and a sound mind. Therefore in public worship everything is to be done decently and in order. Speaking or teaching to speak with unintelligible sounds is not consistent with such order. The language of worship is to be the language of the people. All communication in worship is to be experienced with understanding (I Corinthians 14:6-12).

Life in the Spirit is characterized by pure love. The gifts of the Spirit are to be accompanied by the fruit of the Spirit. Every gift of the Spirit is exercised with the love and compassion of Christ. Unkind critical attitudes and schism in the church are evidences of the flesh (Galatians 5:13-15).

TRUST

¶306. Trust is confidence in and utter reliance upon God (II Corinthians 3:4-5; I Timothy 4:10). Trust includes full acceptance of the promises of God, complete dependence on Christ's sacrifice for salvation, and unconditional commitment to the will of God. God's grace and blessings are open to those who turn to him with firm reliance on his integrity, love, and ability.

Christians experience God's loving care and guidance as they trust and follow him (Ephesians 3:12). When they think they are sufficient unto themselves they become frustrated by trying to do for themselves what God wants to do for them. Self-sufficiency is inconsistent with perfect trust (I Timothy 6:17).

ASSURANCE

¶ 307. God gives assurance of salvation and peace of heart to all who repent and put their faith in him (Romans 5:1). The Holy Spirit witnesses to their own spirits that they are forgiven of their sins and adopted into the family of God Romans 8:16).

The Christian has peace with God through Jesus Christ because his guilt is taken away and his fear of judgment is removed (Hebrews 6:11; 10:22). God continues to give assurance to believers through the Scriptures, the conscious presence of the Holy Spirit, and love for and fellowship with other Christians (I John 3:14).

GROWING IN CHRIST

¶ 308. The Christian has a new relationship with God and a new life in Christ by the power of the Holy Spirit. The joy of this new life in Christ may for a time obscure the need for growing up in Christ, often referred to as Christian maturity. The new Christian must ultimately choose between growth and decline.

The Bible is the Christian's growth manual. It must be taken seriously, read, and studied for meaning. God will speak to the growing Christian through its pages if he is listening. The value and meaning of life are found in this book. Scripture is a means of cleansing and changing attitudes and acts.

The growing Christian is increasingly sensitive to both good and evil, steadily learning to distinguish between them. The Holy Spirit will guide him, in harmony with the

Scriptures, and he must be alert to the Spirit's directives, immediately resisting temptation and responding to God's call to higher living.

Maturity involves personal development which yields growing respect for one's self and for others. Respect for others necessitates self-respect. The Ten Commandments, summarized into two by Jesus, teach the nature of respect in the growth of the moral person. The quality of a Christian relationship to others affects the quality of his own life. Growth in Christ requires readiness to mend relationships both with God and others (James 5:16).

Growth in Christ involves responsibility for the well-being of others, all of whom are loved by God and made in his image. Christians need to love and to be loved. They will express their love both by deeds of kindness and by personal words of witness that Christ is the embodiment of God's love and the Savior of the world.

Maturity in Christ should develop adequacy for life and a concern for the transformation of the world according to God's will. Trusting in God and sustained by the Holy Spirit, the Christian will replace attitudes of defeat and futility with those of courage and confidence.

Prayer is an indispensable means of growth toward Christlikeness. In prayer the Christian talks and listens, confesses and adores, asks and thanks. It should be as conversation, avoiding artificial phrases and tones. Sincere prayer changes the supplicant and often his circumstances (James 5:16). The Bible teaches that both individual and group praying are effective for those who are in Christ. Prayer takes us beyond ourselves and emphasizes our dependence on God. Both prayer and Bible study should be regular, without becoming mere rituals (Psalm 119:11, 105).

The growing Christian finds his proper environment in the fellowship of believers. He does not live in independence from the body of Christ. Worship requires a proper attitude toward God. It involves the believer's active participation. He must prepare his mind and spirit for communication with God. The sincere follower of Christ reaches out to God in praise, thanksgiving, dedication, confession, faith, and service. As a part of the body of Christ he must involve himself in corporate church worship as well as in the other ministries of the church. Support, insight, inspiration, and discipline are fruits of fellowship. Small group participation is a means of grace and growth.

Growth comes with the acceptance of duty in the life of the church. The Holy Spirit provides every Christian with talents which can be developed for the common good. The use of these talents is a means of growth. God ministers to him as he engages in activities pleasing to the Lord.

CHRISTIAN CONDUCT

¶ **325.** We expect that all who are received into the membership of the church shall be examples of Christian conduct. They should avoid evil of every kind and do good in every way possible as set forth in the covenant (Pars. 158-160). They should diligently apply themselves to abide by the principles set forth in the following statements.

HUMAN RIGHTS

¶ **326.** We believe in and are committed to the worth of all persons regardless of differences of sex, race, color, or other distinctions (Acts 10:34-35). We are pledged to respect the inherent rights of, and to seek justice for, every person in any society or government where we may live as citizens.

Our commitment is based on the creation of all persons in the image of God (Genesis 1:26); the respect of all persons implicit in the commands of God through Moses and in the summary of the law given by Jesus (Deuteronomy 5:11-21; Matthew 22:36-40); the needs of all persons which Jesus placed above institutions and to which he ministered without discrimination; the redemption of all persons by the act of

God as recorded in the Bible; the love of all persons as shown in the cross of Christ (John 15:12; 3:16; Romans 5:8).

We are therefore pledged to active concern wherever and whenever human beings are demeaned, depersonalized, or subjected to demonic forces in the world, whether by persons or institutions (Galatians 3:28; Mark 2:27). We are committed to give meaning and significance to every person as God grants us the capability.

As Christians we must grow in awareness, not only of the rights and needs of others but of our own proneness to prejudice.

CHRISTIAN CITIZENSHIP

¶ **327.** The Christian is a citizen of the kingdom of God and also of this world. He receives benefits and bears responsibilities from both relationships. His first allegiance is to God, but that does not release him from responsibilities to his own country if they do not conflict with the clear teachings of the Scriptures (Romans 13:1-7). He should pray for "all who are in high positions" (I Timothy 2:2) and should "be subject for the Lord's sake to every human institution" (I Peter 2:13). He should actively participate in civic life by involvement in constructive efforts for the improvement of social, cultural, and educational standards (Matthew 5:13-16); by opposition to degrading influences (II Peter 2:4-10); and by the exercise of his right to vote.

CIVIL OATHS

¶ **328.** Vain and rash swearing is forbidden by our Lord (Matthew 5:34; James 5:12). However, we hold that the Christian religion does not prohibit the taking of an oath where it is required by a public official. In every case, the Christian must speak in justice and in truth (Jeremiah 4:1-2; Ephesians 4:25).

MARRIAGE AND DIVORCE

¶ **329.** 1. We believe that from the beginning God

33

intends for mankind's good that marriage should be a lifelong union of a man and a woman (Mark 10:6-9). Marriage is an honorable and proper setting for the full expression of the heterosexual nature of mankind (Hebrews 13:4), and the church has no authority to forbid marriage (I Timothy 4:3). This abiding union has been used by the apostles to illustrate the holy relationship between Christ and his church (Ephesians 5:23-33).

2. We do not prohibit our people from marrying persons who are not members of our church provided such persons give evidence of being converted to God. Marriage of our members to unbelievers should be discouraged in accord with the apostle's command, "Do not be mismated with unbelievers" (II Corinthians 6:14). In general, Christian youth ought not to marry without the consent of their parents. All should counsel with their Christian leaders before entering into marriage.

3. We do not permit members of the church to separate, to divorce, and to remarry except in those cases which accord with the counsel of the Word of God.

   a. Whereas forgiveness and reconciliation would be the ideal solution and should be sought, a member of the church may divorce an adulterous mate and remarry (Matthew 5:31-32; 19:3-11).

   b. The husband and wife when both are members of the church may be permitted to separate when an otherwise impossible situation is destroying the peace of the home. In such cases neither partner may remarry. The way to reconciliation must be kept open (I Corinthians 7:10-11).

   c. When one marriage partner is a Christian and the other a nonbeliever, the Christian may not for that reason divorce the unchristian mate (I Corinthians 7:12, 13), for Christian love may redeem the unbeliever and unite the home in Christ (I Corinthians 7:16).

d. When a marriage partner deserts the wife or husband, a desertion which leads subsequently to divorce, the Christian brother or sister who is not in violation of the church's position regarding divorce is no longer bound by the marriage and may remarry (I Corinthians 7:15).

e. A member of the church will be considered guilty of adultery if the member marries one who has divorced a previous mate on any other than biblical grounds (Matthew 5:32; Mark 10:11-12; Luke 16:18; I Corinthians 7:15).

4. The church must seek to be redemptive in all stituations. We believe all sin except blasphemy against the Holy Spirit may be forgiven (Matthew 12:31). Therefore, those persons who have been involved in divorce on other than scriptural grounds prior to their Christian conversion and application for membership shall not for that reason be barred from membership, even though they are remarried.

5. Our ministers shall not officiate at the marriage of any person who is under eighteen years of age, unless the parents or guardians be present or have given written consent, and unless at least two witnesses who know the contracting persons be present. They shall refuse to officiate at the marriage of divorced persons, unless furnished with satisfactory evidence that they are not in violation of the church's position regarding divorce.

USE OF DRUGS

¶ **330.** 1. We believe the Christian presents his body to God as a living sacrifice (Romans 12:1) and accepts responsibility to keep himself as a temple of the Holy Spirit (I Corinthians 6:19-20). He does not knowingly or willfully abuse his body or mind by what he eats, drinks, or does (I Corinthians 10:31). He avoids the use of tobacco, alcoholic beverages, and other self-destructive drugs.

2. Crime, accidental death, broken home, and job loss

studies show close relationship to the use of drugs including alcoholic beverages. Therefore, the Christian should not knowingly give his vote or influence to elect any person to public office who will use his official or personal influence to legalize the traffic in drugs of any type other than for medicinal purposes.

SIMPLICITY OF LIFE

¶ **331.** While customs and man-made standards change from age to age throughout the world, we recognize that there are certain scriptural principles which should govern Christians in their attitudes and conduct. Whatever we buy, use, or wear should help us in winning others to Christ, edifying the body of Christ, and glorifying Christ (I Corinthians 10:31-33).

Those biblical principles which should govern Christians in their choice and purchase of all possessions include simplicity, modesty, purity, propriety, humility, and economy. Christians should avoid extravagance, endeavoring to be clean, tidy, attractive, modest representatives of Christ (I Timothy 2:8-10; I Peter 3:1-5).

The principles of simplicity of life should be considered when we purchase or build or furnish a home, buy a car, select clothes, shop for food, and in all other matters.

STEWARDSHIP OF POSSESSIONS

¶ **332.** The Scriptures teach the right and responsibility of private ownership. The Christian holds title to possessions under civil law, but he regards all he has as the property of God entrusted to him as a steward. Although he may accumulate goods he lays not up *for himself* treasures on earth (Matthew 6:19-20; Luke 12:16-21) but gives liberally for the needs of others and the ministry of the church (II Corinthians 8:1-5; 9:6-13).

SECRET SOCIETIES

¶ **333.** 1. The Christian's supreme loyalty must be to

Jesus Christ who is Lord (Romans 14:9; Acts 2:36). In all his associations the Christian must keep himself free to follow Christ and obey the will of God (II Corinthians 6:14-18). Therefore we require every member to avoid solemn bonds of fellowship with unbelievers which may confuse his identity and cloud his witness.

2. Those voluntary associations which demand an oath, affirmation, promise of secrecy, or a secret password as conditions of membership are to be considered secret societies. In contradiction to the teaching of Christ and the New Testament these societies require pledges and vows which bind the future actions of those who join (Matthew 5:34-37). The Christian, therefore, who forswears his unreserved loyalty to any secret society is in direct conflict with his unconditional surrender to Jesus Christ as Lord. The Christian must keep himself free to follow the will of the Lord in all things.

3. Most secret societies are religious in nature. Prayers are offered, hymns are sung, and members engage in acts of worship before an altar. Chaplains are chosen to lead in worship and to conduct funerals. But the worship of these societies is unitarian, not Christian; the religion is moralistic, not redemptive; and the ends are humanistic, not evangelical (Acts 4:12). We insist, therefore, that those who are members of our church refrain from membership in all secret societies and that those who unite with the church resign from active membership in any lodge or secret order previously joined.

4. We do not require those who become members of the church to cease all payments necessary to keep in force insurance benefits previously contracted through lodge membership.

EMPLOYER AND EMPLOYEE

¶ **334.** 1. All persons have the right to gainful and meaningful employment irrespective of sex, race, color, national origin, or creed (Romans 10:12).

2. We recognize the right of employees to organize for the purpose of seeking in a proper way their betterment in labor, industry, and business. Oath-bound secret pacts or acts of violence designed to violate or defend these rights cannot be condoned. We also recognize the right of the individual to remain independent of organization.

3. In labor relations, justice is an indispensable ingredient in the Christian's code of ethics. It is a part of God's nature and of his norm for us. The Christian concern for justice is a peculiar one: it is primarily a concern to do justice and only secondarily a concern to obtain justice. This norm is equally applicable to employer and employee (Ephesians 6:5-9; Colossians 3:22 — 4:1).

4. The Christian should not view management and labor as ultimately hostile opponents. He should not bring distrust and hostility with him either to his place of work or to the negotiating table. There is no place in the Christian ethic for exploitation, for using people as a means to a selfish end, or for seeing them primarily as economic units. He does not use the adversary system for rigid confrontation, but he supports and implements a problem-solving approach.

5. Our people should endeavor to make their witness effective where they work, remembering that a Christian workman is responsible first to God and then to his employer and the organization (Matthew 7:12; Colossians 3:17).

WAR AND PEACE

¶ **335.** 1. We recognize the sovereign authority of government and the duty of every Christian to reverence the power, to obey the law, and to participate righteously in the administration of lawful order in the nation under whose protection he resides (Matthew 22:21; Romans 13:1-7). Members of our church should bear the responsibilities of good citizenship, and they have the right to act in the enforcement of law and the defense of the peace in accord with the conscience of each person.

2. We believe, however, that military aggression is indefensible as an instrument of national policy and strategy (Isaiah 2:3-4). The destruction of life and property and the deceit and violence necessary to warfare are contrary to the spirit and mind of Jesus Christ (Isaiah 9:6-7; Matthew 5:44-45). It is therefore the duty of every Christian to promote peace and goodwill, to foster the spirit of understanding and mutual trust among all people, and to work with patience for the renunciation of war as a means to the settlement of international disputes (Romans 12:18; 14:19).

3. It is our firm conviction that none of our people should be required to enter military training or to bear arms except in time of national peril and that the consciences of our individual members should be respected (Acts 4:19-20; 5:29). Therefore, we claim exemption from all military service for those who register officially with the church as conscientious objectors to war.

PUBLIC SCHOOLS

¶ **336.** The Free Methodist Church views the education of its youth as a parental responsibility (Deuteronomy 6:5-9; Ephesians 6:4). Part of that responsibility may be delegated to either public or Christian day schools.

The church gives moral support to the public school system. However, we reserve the right of our children and youth to be exempted from participating in dancing, assignments, and other school-related activities which conflict with the moral and social values held by the denomination. When such conflicts arise, we ask that the students' academic standing not be in jeopardy but when necessary other suitable assignments be substituted.

CHRISTIAN FELLOWSHIP

1. CHARACTERISTICS OF THE FELLOWSHIP

¶ **350.** It is our purpose to encourage the development

and maintenance of warm, caring fellowship in all our societies. The holy love portrayed by the New Testament writers should be our conscious goal and our mark of identity. It is not enough that we attend services of worship with each other. We must know other Christians well enough to share our strengths and weaknesses, our insights and ignorances, our joys and sorrows, that together we may grow up into Christ. Understanding, forgiveness, mutual discipline, and assistance must be found in each of our societies if we are to fulfill the desire of Christ for his church. Let pastor and people show mutual concern that each person realizes his full potential in both character and service. Let pastor and people develop appropriate means for fostering fellowship in the church. Let us remind ourselves that the world will be won, not only by the proclamation of the gospel, but by the availability of a warm and redeeming fellowship.

We should be deeply sensitive to the evil of division in principle, spirit, or practice, and to the dreadful consequences to ourselves and the church. If we are united, what can stand before us? If we divide, we shall destroy ourselves, the work of God, and the souls of our people.

RECEPTION INTO PREPARATORY MEMBERSHIP

¶ 351. (Ritual other than questions and answers is optional.)

[Those who are to be received as preparatory members shall be called forward by name, and the minister, addressing the people, shall say:]

Dearly beloved, that none may be admitted into the Free Methodist Church without instruction, we receive persons who seek fellowship with us into preparatory membership, during which they may be properly instructed, and also give proof, both to themselves and to the church, of the sincerity and depth of their convictions and of the strength and purpose of their desire to lead a new life.

[Then addressing the persons seeking admission as preparatory members, the minister shall say:]

Beloved in the Lord, you have by the grace of God made

your decision to follow Christ and to serve him. Your confidence in so doing is to be based, not on any notion of fitness or worthiness in yourselves, but on the gracious promise of God, through our Lord Jesus Christ, who loved us and gave himself for us.

That the church may know your purpose, you will answer the following questions:

1. Do you have the assurance that God has forgiven your sins through faith in Jesus Christ?

Answer: I have.

2. Are you willing to receive membership instruction as offered by our church?

Answer: I am.

3. Have you received Christian baptism?

Answer: Yes or no.

If not, will you receive this sacrament at a duly appointed time?

Answer: Yes.

4. You have been won to Christ. Will you endeavor to win others to Christ and the church?

Answer: I will.

[Then shall the minister say:]

On behalf of the Free Methodist Church, and in the hope that you will go forward to complete membership therein, I extend to you a cordial welcome.

[Then shall the minister offer extempore prayer.]

¶ 352. Preparatory members shall not be continued longer than two years on the membership roll, in that relation, without a two-thirds vote of the official board that circumstances warrant a continuation for a longer period.

ADMISSION INTO JUNIOR MEMBERSHIP

¶ 355. (Ritual other than questions and answers is optional.)

[Those who are to be received as junior members shall be called forward by name, and the minister shall say:]

Beloved, our Lord Jesus, by his Holy Word has expressly given to everyone who believes in him a place in his kingdom

41

and church. Before you are admitted into the church, it becomes my duty to inquire of you as to your purpose of mind and heart.

1. Do you believe that Jesus Christ has forgiven your sins and is now your Savior?

Answer: I do.

2. Have you received Christian baptism?*

Answer: Yes or no.

If not, will you consent to be baptized at such a time as your pastor may choose?

Answer: Yes.

3. Will you faithfully attend your pastor's class of instruction on living the Christian life and serving God through your church?

Answer: I will.

4. Will you be loyal to the Free Methodist Church and uphold it in your prayers, your presence, your gifts, and your service?

Answer: I will.

---

* Those received into junior membership who have been baptized in infancy are required to affirm the baptismal vows. See Paragraph 903.

5. Will you endeavor to show your friends by your life what it means to be a Christian, and will you do your best to win them to Christ?

Answer: I will.

Optional:

[Here the minister may offer an extempore prayer. Then those to be received as junior members shall kneel, and the minister, laying his hands upon each of them in turn, shall say:]

I receive you into the fellowship of the Free Methodist Church as a junior member. May God confirm you in the faith and fellowship of all true disciples of Jesus Christ. Amen.

¶ 356. All members under sixteen years of age shall be known as junior members. They shall not be counted in the allocation of financial goals by the annual or general conference. Their number shall be kept in a separate column in the statistical report. They are not eligible to vote in business meetings.

The names of junior members shall be reviewed by the official board at least once each year, with a view to character cultivation and Christian nurture, but in no case shall any change in their membership status be made until they reach their sixteenth birthday, other than the provisions in Paragraph 153.

Upon reaching the sixteenth birthday, junior members shall be approved by the official board either for full membership or for transfer to the preparatory membership roll. To be admitted to full voting membership, they must answer satisfactorily the questions for full membership and receive a three-fourths vote of approval by the members present and voting.

Junior members shall be reported in a separate column in the *Yearbook*.

ADMISSION INTO FULL MEMBERSHIP

¶ **360.** (Ritual other than questions and answers is optional.)

None shall be received into full membership unless he gives evidence of a renewed heart by living up to the requirements of the general rules; has received at least three months' instruction for full membership as required by the General Conference; has been baptized, and, if baptized in infancy, has publicly assented to the baptismal covenant; has been approved by the official board of the church; and gives affirmative answers to the following questions for full membership, before a public meeting of the church.

[Those who are to be received into full membership shall be called forward by name, and, the minister, addressing the people, shall say:]

Dearly beloved, the church is of God and will be preserved to the end of time for the promotion of his worship and the due administration of his word and ordinances, the maintenance of Christian fellowship and discipline, the edification of believers, and the conversion of the lost. All, of every age and station, stand in need of the means of grace which it alone supplies.

Into this holy fellowship the persons before you, who have received the Sacrament of Baptism, who have learned the nature of these privileges and these duties, and who have also been instructed in the teachings and the mission of the Free Methodist Church, come seeking admission as adult members in full connection. We now propose in the fear of God to question them as to their faith and purpose, that you may know that they are proper persons to be admitted into this church.

[Then, addressing those seeking admission, the minister shall say:]

Beloved in the Lord, you are come hither seeking union with the Free Methodist Church. We rejoice that you are minded to undertake the privileges and the duties of membership in this church. Before you are fully admitted thereto, you shall here publicly renew your vows, confess your faith, and declare your purpose, by answering the following questions:

1. Have you now the assurance of the Holy Spirit that your sins are forgiven through faith in Jesus Christ?

2. Do you now experience the fullness of the Holy Spirit with his cleansing of heart and empowerment for service?

(If the candidate should answer, "No," then ask: Will you seek his fullness through study, counsel, and prayer?)

3. Is it your intention to serve God by the full use of the abilities he has given you?

4. Do you believe the Holy Scriptures to be the revealed will of God containing all things necessary to salvation through faith in Jesus Christ?

5. Do you accept the Articles of Religion, the Membership Covenant, and the Organization and Government of the Free Methodist Church, and will you endeavor to live in harmony with them?

6. As a member of the Free Methodist Church, will you be faithful in attendance, prayer, and fellowship with the pastor and fellow-members of the church?

7. Will you practice the principles of Christian stewardship, giving freely of your time, talents, and possessions to Christ and his church?

[Here the minister shall introduce each candidate by name to the
congregation, and shall continue as follows:]

You, my fellow-members of this congregation, have heard
the vows of these who have completed the requirements for
full membership in the Free Methodist Church. Let us indicate
our desire to welcome them into our fellowship. (The method
shall be left to the discretion of the minister in charge, and
this shall fulfill the requirements of Par. 151, Sec. 4, and Par.
361, Sec. 1.)

[Here the minister may offer an extempore prayer.]

This is optional:

[Then those to be received into full membership shall kneel, and the minister,
laying his hands upon each of them in turn, shall say:]

_____, I receive you into the fellowship of the Free
Methodist Church. May the Lord confirm you in the faith and
fellowship of the true disciples of Jesus Christ. Amen.

[Those being received shall rise, and the minister, addressing the candidates,
shall say:]

We rejoice to recognize you as members of the Free
Methodist Church and bid you welcome to all its privileges;
and in token of our brotherly love we give you the right hand
of fellowship and pray that you may be numbered with his
people here and with his saints in glory everlasting. May the
church be a blessing to you, and may you be a blessing to the
church.

[Then shall the minister say to the congregation:]

Brethren, I commend to your love and care these persons
whom we this day recognize as members of our church. Do
all in your power to strengthen their faith, confirm their hope,
and perfect them in love.

¶ **361.** 1. The person giving satisfactory answers to the
questions in Paragraph 360 shall, with consent of three-
fourths of the members present, be admitted to all the
privileges of membership.

2. Any person in good standing in any evangelical church
may be received into full membership upon meeting the other

requirements of this chapter (see Par. 360), and having received adequate instruction for membership in our church, without having been a preparatory member.

CHRISTIAN WORSHIP

PREAMBLE

¶ 375. We believe rites and ceremonies of the church are to be accorded respect. One should not through his own private judgment willfully and purposefully disregard the rites of the church to which he belongs. Such rites are not the same in all places or churches. There have always been differences, reflecting the diversity of times and countries and the customs of men. Therefore, we acknowledge the right of every denomination to change and ordain rites and ceremonies, for the edification of all. But let nothing be ordained against God's Word.

¶ 376. Public worship in our churches shall seek a balance between freedom and form. Preaching shall be emphasized as a means of edifying believers and converting sinners. All public worship shall be in the language of the people.

ORDER OF PUBLIC WORSHIP

¶ 377. The Sunday morning corporate worship service should provide four basic results: (1) to provide opportunity for the praise of God; (2) to give worshipers insight into the will of God; (3) to lead individuals to commit themselves personally to God's revealed will; and (4) to strengthen the dedicated person to perform the will of God. To accomplish these desired results, each service should include congregational singing, reading from the Scriptures, pastoral prayer, the Lord's Prayer, and preaching. The apostolic benediction is recommended for dismissing the congregation.

Other services shall include congregational singing, prayer, reading from the Scriptures, and preaching. On occasion, sharing, healing of human hurts, and other forms of worship may be used. The order of services should avoid routine by providing fitting variations in worship forms within the limitations of propriety, the Scriptures, and specific rituals when used (Chapter IX).

The minister shall insist on reverence and a worshipful attitude before, during, and after worship and shall himself be an example.

MUSIC

¶ **378.** Qualified persons whose character and life reveal the scriptural principles and support the standards of the Free Methodist Church shall be selected to lead the singing in public worship and, where instrumental music is in use, play the instrument.

The pastor is responsible to provide for the cultivation of sacred music and to guard against complexity and formality in singing. Singing is a part of divine worship in which all persons present should unite. Congregational music shall not be subordinated to special music. Hymns fitting to the occasion should be chosen, and seldom should more than four or five stanzas of one hymn be used. The Free Methodist hymnal is expected to be used in the morning worship service.

The use of instrumental music is the decision of the local church or other ecclesiastical unit conducting worship.

The purpose of music in divine service is to inspire and to sustain worship. Vocal and instrumental music used in the service shall seek to contribute to reverence and exalted worship and not the display of talent, however excellent.

LOVE FEAST

¶ **379.** The love feast is one of the fascinating yet least understood aspects of the rites of the early church. John Wesley reintroduced it to millions of modern Christians, to whom it proved (and still proves) an inspiring means of grace. Historically, Free Methodists observed the love feast at least once in three months.

Love feasts are characterized by the singing of hymns, opportunity for testimony, extemporaneous prayer, and the breaking of bread in symbolizing the meals shared by the early Christians. The love feast is not to be confused with the Sacrament of the Lord's Supper.

CHRISTIAN GROWTH GROUPS (CLASSES)

¶ 380. In the year 1739 eight or ten persons sought the spiritual counsel and guidance of Mr. Wesley in London. They asked that he spend time with them in prayer and the study of the Scriptures. Thus began the Methodist United Societies. Members saw themselves as "a company of persons having the form and seeking the power of godliness, united in order to pray together, to receive the word of exhortation, and to watch over one another in love, that they may help each other to work out their salvation."

For the purpose of Christian nurture and more intimate fellowship, societies were divided into classes, not exceeding twelve in number. These classes proved to be one of the most important features in the perpetuation of the Methodist revival. The practice of Christian nurture through small groups has always been regarded as a vital feature of the Free Methodist Church.

Christian growth groups should be formed within the congregation for the careful oversight of the members and the confirmation of seekers in the assurance of God's forgiveness in Christ. Membership in the groups ideally should be not more than twelve. A leader shall be chosen by the group, and the pastor may nominate. The groups should meet in a convenient location on a regular schedule.

Group meetings should be devoted to meaningful, creative prayer; the study of the Scriptures; the sharing of needs, aspirations, and victories; and fellowship in Christian love. Persons not yet believers should be invited into the fellowship as they desire to learn of Christ.

Leaders of small groups should be chosen carefully. They

shall be members of the Free Methodist Church, persons of mature Christian faith and experience. They should have a good understanding of the Scriptures and agree fully with the doctrines and practices of the church.

PART TWO

Faith and Life
(From Words of John Wesley)

The Character of a Methodist
(Excerpts)

The distinguishing marks of a Methodist are not his opinions of any sort. His assenting to this or that scheme of religion, his embracing any particular set of notions, his espousing the judgment of one man or of another, are all quite wide of the point. Whosoever, therefore, imagines that a Methodist is a man of such or such an opinion is grossly ignorant of the whole affair; he mistakes the truth totally. We believe, indeed, that "all Scripture is given by the inspiration of God." . . . We believe the written word of God to be the only and sufficient rule both of Christian faith and practice. . . . We believe Christ to be the eternal, supreme God. . . . But as to all opinions which do not strike at the root of Christianity, we think and let think. . . .

Nor do we desire to be distinguished by actions, customs, or usages of an indifferent nature. Our religion does not lie in doing what God has not enjoined, or abstaining from what he hath not forbidden. It does not lie in the form of our apparel, in the posture of our body, or the covering of our heads; nor yet in abstaining from marriage, or from meats and drinks, which are all good if received with thanksgiving. . . .

"What, then, is the mark? Who is a Methodist, according to your own account?" *I answer:* A Methodist is one who has "the love of God shed abroad in his heart by the Holy Spirit given unto him"; one who "loves the Lord his God with all his heart, and with all his soul, and with all his mind, and with all his strength." God is the joy of his heart, and the desire of his soul. . . .

He is therefore happy in God, yea, always happy, as having in him "a well of water springing up into everlasting life" and overflowing his soul with peace and joy. "Perfect love" having now "cast out fear," he "rejoices evermore." He "rejoices in the Lord always," even "in God his Saviour"; and in the Father, "through our Lord Jesus Christ, by whom he hath now received the atonement." . . . For "he that believeth, hath the witness" of this "in himself"; being now the son of God by faith. "Because he is a son, God hath sent forth the Spirit of his Son into his heart, crying, Abba, Father!" And "the Spirit itself beareth witness with his spirit, that he is a child of God." . . .

Indeed he "prays without ceasing." . . . Not that he is always in the house of prayer. . . . Neither is he always on his knees or on his face before the Lord his God. . . . But at all times the language of his heart is this: ". . . unto thee is my heart, and my silence speaketh unto thee." And this is true prayer, and this alone. But his heart is ever lifted up to God, at all times and in all places.

. . . This commandment is written in his heart, "That he who loveth God, love his brother also." And he accordingly loves his neighbor as himself; he loves every man as his own soul. His heart is full of love to all mankind, to every child of "the Father of the spirits of all flesh.". . .

He is "pure in heart." The love of God has purified his heart from all revengeful passions, from envy, malice, and wrath, from every unkind temper or malign affection. It hath cleansed him from pride and haughtiness of spirit, whereof alone cometh contention. And he hath now "put on kindness, humbleness of mind, meekness, long-suffering"; so that he "forbears and forgives, if he had a quarrel against any; even as God in Christ hath forgiven him." . . .

His one desire is the one design of his life, namely, "not to do his own will, but the will of Him that sent him." His own intention at all times and in all things is, not to please himself, but Him whom his soul loveth. He has a single eye. And because "his eye is single, his whole body is full of light."

. . . As he loves God, so he keeps His commandments; not

only some, or most of them, but all, from the least to the greatest.... Whatever God has forbidden, he avoids; whatever God hath enjoined, he doeth....

All the commandments of God he accordingly keeps, and that with all his might. For his obedience is in proportion to his love, the source from whence it flows. And therefore, loving God with all the heart, he serves him with all his strength. He continually presents his soul and body a living sacrifice, holy, acceptable to God; entirely and without reserve devoting himself, all he has, and all he is, to His glory.... His one invariable rule is this, "whatsoever ye do, in word or deed, do all in the name of the Lord Jesus, giving thanks to God and the Father by him."

... He knows that vice does not lose its nature, though it becomes ever so fashionable; and remembers that "every man is to give an account of himself to God." He cannot, therefore, "follow" even "a multitude to do evil." He cannot "fare sumptuously every day," or "make provisions for the flesh to fulfill the lusts thereof." ...

As he has time, he "does good unto all men"; unto neighbors and strangers, friends and enemies: and that in every possible kind; not only to their bodies, by "feeding the hungry, clothing the naked, visiting those that are sick or in prison"; but much more does he labor to do good to their souls, as of the ability which God giveth....

These are the principles and practices of our sect; these are the marks of a true Methodist. By these alone does he so desire to be distinguished from other men. If any man say, "Why, these are only the common, fundamental principles of Christianity!" Thou hast said; so I mean: that is the very truth.... Whosoever is what I preach ... is a Christian, not in name only, but in heart and in life. He is inwardly and outwardly conformed to the will of God, as revealed in the written word. He thinks, speaks, and lives, according to the method laid down in the revelation of Jesus Christ. His soul is renewed after the image of God, in righteousness and in all true holiness. And having the mind that was in Christ, he so walks as Christ also walked.

By these marks, by these fruits of a living faith, do we labor to distinguish ourselves from the unbelieving world, from all those whose minds or lives are not according to the gospel of Christ. But from real Christians, of whatsoever denomination they be, we earnestly desire not to be distinguished at all; not from any who sincerely follow after what they know they have not yet attained. . . .

Is thy heart right, as my heart is with thine? I ask no further question. If it be, give me thine hand. . . . Dost thou love and serve God? It is enough. I give thee the right hand of fellowship.

— "The Character of a Methodist"

Wesley Testifies (Before Aldersgate)

I have thrown up my friends, reputation, ease, country. I have put my life in my hands, wandering into strange lands. I have given up my body to be devoured by the deep, parched with heat, consumed by toil and weariness or whatever God shall be pleased to bring upon me. *But does all this . . . make me acceptable to God?* Does all I ever did, or can know, say, give, do, or suffer, justify me in his sight? The faith I want is a sure trust and confidence in God that through the merits of Christ *my* sins are forgiven, and I am reconciled to the favor of Christ. . . . I want that faith which none can have without knowing that he hath it.

— Journal, Jan. 29, 1738, on ship, returning to England from America

---

I want that faith which St. Paul recommends to all the world, especially in his Epistle to the Romans — that faith which enables everyone that hath it to cry out: "I live not, but Christ liveth in me; and the life which I now live, I live by faith in the Son of God who loved me and gave himself for me."

— Journal, Jan. 29, 1738

The anthem that John Wesley heard at St. Paul's, London, on the day of his great experience:

> "Out of the deeps have I called unto thee,
> O Lord, Lord, hear my voice:
> O let thine ears consider well
> The voice of my complaint.
> If thou, Lord, wilt be extreme
> To mark what is done amiss,
> O Lord, who may abide it?
> For there is mercy with thee;
> Therefore shalt thou be feared.
> O Israel, trust in the Lord,
> For with the Lord there is mercy,
> And with him is plenteous redemption.
> And he shall redeem Israel from all his sins."

— Adapted from Psalm 103:1-4, 7-8

About Aldersgate

"In the evening I went very unwillingly to a society in Aldersgate Street, where one was reading Luther's *Preface to the Epistle to the Romans*. About a quarter before nine, while he was describing the change which God works in the heart through faith in Christ, I felt my heart strangely warmed. I felt I did trust in Christ, Christ alone, for salvation; and an assurance was given me that he had taken away my sins, even mine, and saved me from the law of sin and death."

— *Journal,* May 24, 1738

"The testimony of the Spirit is an inward impression on the soul, whereby the Spirit of God directly witnesses to my spirit, that I am a child of God; that Jesus Christ has loved *me,* and given himself for *me;* and that all my sins are blotted out and I, *even I,* am reconciled to God."

— Sermon, *The Witness of the Spirit"*

I have seen very many persons changed in a moment from the spirit of fear, horror, despair to a spirit of love, joy, and peace; and from sinful desire to a pure desire of doing the will of God. These are matters of fact, whereof I am almost daily an eye or ear witness.
— *Journal,* May 20, 1739

I find scarcely any temptation from any *thing* in the world; my danger is from persons.
— Letter, undated, except May 11

I am exceedingly afraid of covetousness, lest it should steal unawares either upon myself or my friends.
— April 26, 1777

I seek two things in this world — truth and love. Whoever assists me in this search is a friend indeed, whether personally known or unknown to me.
— June 28, 1755

A Prayer of John Wesley
I Give Thee Myself

To thee, O God, Father, Son, and Holy Spirit, my Creator, Redeemer, and Sanctifier, I give up myself entirely. May I no longer serve myself, but thee, all the days of my life.

I give thee my understanding. May it be my only care to know thee, thy perfections, thy works, and thy will. Let all things else be as dross unto me, for the excellency of this knowledge, and let me silence all reasonings against whatsoever thou teachest me, who canst neither deceive nor be deceived.

I give thee my will. May I have no will of my own. Whatsoever thou willest, may I will, and that only. May I will thy glory in all things, as thou dost, and make that my end in every thing. May I ever say with the Psalmist, "Whom have I in heaven but thee? and there is none upon earth that I desire beside thee." May I delight to do thy will, O God, and rejoice to suffer it. Whatever threatens me, let me say, "It is the Lord; let him do what seemeth him good"; and whatever befalls me, let me give thanks, since it is thy will concerning me.

I give thee my affections. Do thou dispose of them all. Be thou my love, my fear, my joy; and may nothing have any share in them, but with respect to thee and for thy sake. What thou lovest, may I love; what thou hatest, may I hate; and that in such measures as thou art pleased to prescribe me.

I give thee my body. May I glorify thee with it, and preserve it holy, fit for thee, O God, to dwell in. May I neither indulge it, nor use too much rigour toward it; but keep it, as far as in me lies, healthy, vigorous, and active, and fit to do thee all manner of service which thou shalt call for.

I give thee all my wordly goods. May I prize them and use them only for thee. May I faithfully restore to thee, in the poor, all thou hast intrusted me with, above the necessaries of life; and be content to part with them too, whenever thou, my Lord, shall require them at my hands.

I give thee my credit and reputation. May I never value it, but only in respect of thee; nor endeavour to maintain it, but as it may do thee service and advance thy honour in the world.

I give thee myself and my all. Let me look upon myself to be nothing, and to have nothing, out of thee. Be thou the sole disposer and governor of myself and all; be thou my portion and my all.

O my God and my all, when hereafter I shall be tempted to break this solemn engagement, when I shall be pressed to conform to the world and to the company and customs that surround me, may my answer be: "I am not my own; I am not for myself, not for the world, but for my God. I will give unto God the things which are God's. God, be merciful to me a sinner."

— "A Collection of Forms of Prayer" — for "Thursday Evening"

HOLINESS

"And what do you think holiness is?

"It is purity both of heart and life.

"It is the mind that was in Christ, enabling us to walk as he also walked.

"It is loving God with all our heart; the loving our neighbor, every man, as ourselves.

"It is the doing to all men, in every point, as we would they should do unto us."

— "A Word to a Condemned Malefactor"

"I would have you not almost but altogether a Christian.... You cannot be content with less. You cannot be satisfied with right notions; neither with harmlessness; no, nor yet with barely external religion, how exact soever it be. Neither will you be content with a taste of inward religion....

"A taste of love cannot suffice,
Your soul for all his fulness cries."

— Letter, dated May 8, 1774

We have but one point in view: to be altogether Christians, scriptural, rational Christians. For which we well know, not only the world, but the *almost* Christians, will never forgive us. From these, therefore, if you join heart and hand with us, you are to expect neither justice nor mercy.

— Letter, dated only 1767

By Christian perfection, I mean,

1. Loving God with all our heart. Do you object to this?

2. A heart and life all devoted to God. Do you desire less?

3. Regaining the whole image of God. What objection to this?

4. Having all the mind that was in Christ. Is this going too far?

5. Walking uniformly as Christ walked. And this surely no Christian will object to.

If anyone means anything more or anything less by perfection, I have no concern with it.

— *Journal,* June 27, 1769

What is the best proof of our being led by the Spirit? A thorough change and renovation of mind and heart, and the leading a new and holy life.

— "A Farther Appeal"

I have told all the world I am not perfect. . . . I tell you flat, I have not attained the character I draw.

— March 5, 1767

To seek for a particular deliverance from *one* sin only is mere lost labor. If it could be attained, it would be of little worth, for another sin would rise in it place . . . a general deliverance from the guilt and power of all sin is the thing you want and should be continually seeking for.

— June 30, 1764, or January 31, 1764, to John Valton

Q: What is Christian Perfection?

A: The loving God with all our heart, mind, soul, and strength. This implies that no wrong temper, none contrary to love, remains in the soul; and that all the thoughts, words, and actions, are governed by pure love. . . .

Q: How shall we avoid setting perfection too high or too low?

A: By keeping to the Bible, and setting it just as high as the Scripture does.

— "A Plain Account," section 19

Question: What is it to be sanctified?

Answer: To be renewed in the image of God, in righteousness and true holiness.

Q: What is implied in being a perfect Christian?

A: The loving God with all our heart, and mind, and soul.
— "A Plain Account of Christian Perfection," section 17

Entire sanctification, or Christian perfection, is neither more nor less than pure love; love expelling sin, and governing both the heart and life of a child of God. The refiner's fire purges out all that is contrary to love, and that many times by a pleasing smart.
— Feb. 21, 1771

In religion, as in all things else, it is use that brings perfectness.
— June 17, 1774

"Without holiness no man shall see the Lord," shall see the face of God in glory. Nothing under heaven can be more sure than this; "for the mouth of the Lord hath spoken it. And though heaven and earth pass away, yet his word shall not pass away." As well therefore might God fall from heaven, as his word fall to the ground.

None shall live with God, but he who now lives to God; none shall enjoy the glory of God in heaven, but he who bears the image of God on earth; none who are not saved from sin here can be saved from hell hereafter; none can see the kingdom of God above, unless the kingdom of God be in him below.

Whosoever will reign with Christ in heaven must have Christ reigning in him on earth. He must have "that mind in him which was in Christ," enabling him "to walk as Christ also walked."
— From "A Blow at the Root," first paragraph

"The essential part of Christian holiness is giving the heart wholly to God; and certainly we need not lose any degree of that light and love which at first attend this; it is our own infirmity if we do; it is not the will of the Lord concerning us.

"Your present business is not to reason whether you should *call* your experience thus or thus, but to go straight to him that loves you, with all your wants, how great or many soever they are. Then . . . help, while you ask, is given. You have only to receive it by simple faith.

"Nevertheless, you will still be encompassed with numberless infirmities; for you live in an house of clay, and therefore this corruptible body will more or less press down the soul, yet not so as to prevent your rejoicing ever more and having a witness that your heart is all his. You may claim this: it is yours; for Christ is yours. Believe, and feel him near."

— Letter, July 25, 1767

"The *pure in heart* are they whose hearts God hath 'purified even as he is pure' . . . .

"They are, through the power of his grace, purified from pride, by the deepest poverty of spirit; from anger, from every unkind or turbulent passion, by meekness and gentleness; from every desire but to please and enjoy God, to know and love him more and more . . . so that now they love the Lord their God with all their heart, and with all their soul, and mind, and strength.

"But how little has this purity of heart been regarded by the false teachers of all ages! They have taught men barely to abstain from such outward impurities as God hath forbidden by name; but they did not strike at the heart; and . . . inward corruptions. . . .

". . . the pure in heart do more particularly see God. They see his hand ever over them for good . . . numbering the hairs of their heads . . . and disposing all the circumstances of their life according to the depth both of his wisdom and mercy."

— "Upon Our Lord's Sermon on the Mount."

Whether an imagination of already being in a state of perfection is not apt to lead men into spiritual pride? If it be a false imagination, it is spiritual pride. But true Christian perfection is no other than humble love.

— "A Farther Appeal," Part I (5. Q. 2)

PRAYER

Nothing will avail without prayer. Pray, whether you can or not: when you are cheerful, when you are heavy, pray; with many or few words, or none at all. You will surely find an answer of peace.

— June 30, 1764

As long as we steadily watch and pray, we shall not enter into temptations.

— Letter, undated

Fix some part of every day for private exercises. You may acquire the taste which you have not. What is tedious at first will afterwards be pleasant. Whether you like it or not, read and pray daily.

Go straight to God, as a little child, and tell him all your troubles, and hindrances, and doubts; and desire him to turn them all to good.

— Jan. 18, 1774

Continue in private prayer, in spite of all coldness and wanderings, and you shall soon pray without ceasing.

— Letter to Miss D. Perronet, undated

God hath in Scripture ordained prayer, reading or hearing, and the receiving the Lord's Supper as the ordinary means of conveying his grace to man.

"Make me to remember thee on my bed and think upon

thee when I am waking." Thou hast observed me from all the dangers of the day past; thou hast been my support from my youth up until now; "under the shadow of thy wings" let me pass this night in comfort and peace.

— "A Collection of Forms of Prayer" — for "Tuesday Evening"

"In souls filled with love, the desire to please God is a continual prayer."

In Everything, Pray

"On every occasion of uneasiness, we should retire to prayer, that we may give place to the grace and light of God, and then form our resolutions, without being in any pain about what success they may have.

"In the greatest temptations, a single look to Christ, and the barely pronouncing his name, suffices to overcome the wicked one, so it be done with confidence and calmness of spirit.

"God's command to 'pray without ceasing' is founded on the necessity we have of his grace to preserve the life of God in the soul, which can no more subsist one moment without it, than the body can without air.

"Whether we think of, or speak to, God, whether we act or suffer for him — all is prayer, when we have no other object than his love and the desire of pleasing him."

— Plain Account of Christian Perfection

Prayer and thanksgiving is the vital breath
That keeps the spirit of a man from death;
For prayer attracts into the living soul
The life that fills the universal whole;
And giving thanks is breathing forth again
The praise of Him who is the life of men.

— July 18, 1773, John Wesley

BIBLE

". . . I love good men of every church. My ground is the Bible. Yes, I am a Bible bigot. I follow it in all things, both great and small."

— Journal, June 5, 1766

I make it my whole employ, wherever I go, to instill into the people a few favorite tenets — only they are not my own, but his that sent me. And this I do as if the whole of Christianity depended upon them, and all efforts without them were void and vain.

I frequently sum them all up in one: "In Christ Jesus" (that is, according to his gospel) "neither circumcision availeth anything, nor uncircumcision, but faith which worketh by love."

But many times I instill them one by one, under these or the like expressions:

"Thou shalt love the Lord thy God with all thy heart, and with all thy mind, and with all thy soul, and with all thy strength: thou shalt love thy neighbour as thyself;" — as thy own soul; as Christ loved us.

"God is love; and he that dwelleth in love, dwelleth in God, and God in him."

"Love worketh no ill to his neighbour; therefore love is the fulfilling of the law."

"While we have time, let us do good until all men; especially unto them that are of the household of faith."

"Whatsoever ye would that men should do unto you, even so do unto them."

These are my favorite tenets, and have been for many years. O that I could instill them into every soul throughout the land! Ought they not to be instilled with such diligence and zeal, as if the whole of Christianity depended upon them? For who can deny that all efforts toward a Christian life without a thorough experience and practice of these, are utterly vain and ineffectual?

— "A Farther Appeal to Men of Reason and Religion," Part 1 (III. 7)

"In the year 1729 [nine years before Aldersgate] I began not only to read, but to study the Bible, as the one, the only standard of truth, and the only model of pure religion."

— "A Plain Account of Christian Perfection"

"The Bible is the whole and sole rule both of Christian faith and practice."

— Thoughts Upon Methodism"

"Keep close to the Bible, both as to sentiment and expression."

— Letter

"All who desire the grace of God are to wait for it in searching the Scriptures."

— Sermon, "The Means of Grace"

"Faith and salvation include the substance of all the Bible, the marrow, as it were, of the whole Scripture."

— Sermon, "The Scripture Way of Salvation"

CHURCH

"Christianity is essentially a social religion, and to turn it into a solitary one is to destroy it."

Jesus, we look to thee,
　　Thy promised presence claim;
Thou in the midst of us shalt be,
　　Assembled in thy Name:

Thy Name salvation is,
   Which here we come to prove;
Thy Name is life, and health, and peace,
   And everlasting love.

Find satisfaction in Christian companions. It is a blessed thing to have fellow travellers to the New Jerusalem. If you cannot find any, you must make them; for none can travel that road alone.

— Aug. 2, 1789

Take care to improve the Sabbaths, and He will every day stand at your right hand.

— Sept. 22, 1780

LOVE

No scripture can mean that God is not love, or that his mercy is not over all his works.

There is nothing deeper, there is nothing better, in heaven or earth, than love.

— Jan. 17, 1775

Love is all we want: let this fill our hearts, and it is enough.

— Nov. 22, 1769

You have all things in one, the whole of religion contracted to a point in that word, *"Walk in love,* as Christ also loved us and gave himself for us."* All is contained in gentle, humble, patient love.

— Jan. 5, 1772

. . . love is due to all mankind. . . .

But there is a peculiar love which we owe to those that love God. . . .

Though we cannot think alike, may we not love alike? May we not be of one heart, though we are not of one opinion? Without all doubt, we may.

GROWTH IN GRACE

If we grow daily in knowledge and love, it is a good proof that we are born of the Spirit.

— "A Farther Appeal," Part I (III.6)

Grow in grace every hour. . . . Use now all the grace you have . . . but also now expect all the grace you want! This is the secret of heart religion.

— Oct. 14, 1767

Always there should be a gradual growth in grace.

— Nov. 5, 1770

By stirring up the gift of God that is in you, you will find a constant increase of inward life. Labor to be more and more active, more and more devoted to him.

— Dec. 11, 1773

While we live, let us live in earnest.

— April 15, 1788

I see that the whole law of God is holy, just, and good. I know every thought, every temper of my soul *ought to bear God's image* and superscription.

— May 24, 1738, to a friend, on Aldersgate day

Nor steel nor flint alone produces fire,

Nor spark arises till they both conspire:
Nor faith alone, nor works without, is right;
Salvation rises when they both unite.

— July 18,1773

You look inward too much, and upward too little.

— Feb. 16, 1771

MONEY

If the people were more alive to God, they would be more liberal. There is money enough.

— Nov. 3, 1784

"When the Possessor of heaven and earth brought you into being . . . he placed you here, not as a proprietor, but as a steward."

". . . money is not your ultimate end. The treasuring up of gold and silver, for its own sake, is . . . foolish and absurd."

Temporal business need not interrupt your communion with God, though it varies the manner of it.

— May 20, 1771

I save all I can and give all I can; that is, all I have."

— Journal, July 16, 1790. Last entry in Wesley's private *Journal.*

If those who "gain all they can," and "save all they can," will likewise "give all they can," then, the more they gain, the more they will grow in grace, and the more treasure they will lay up in heaven.

MISCELLANEOUS

Do all the good you can,
By all the means you can,
In all the ways you can,
In all the places you can,
To all the people you can,
As long as ever you can.

I hope you lose no opportunity of speaking a word for God, either to them that know him or them that do not."

— Letter to one who was not a preacher, Mrs. Marston, Aug. 26, 1770

Wherever you are, be ready to acknowledge what God has done for your soul; and earnestly exhort all the believers to expect full salvation.

— Oct. 9, 1779

Every believer ought to enjoy life.

— July 27, 1787

Religion has nothing sour, austere, unsociable, unfriendly in it, but, on the contrary, implies the most winning sweetness, the most amiable softness and gentleness.

— March 29, 1783

Sour godliness is the devil's religion.

What kinds of recreation are innocent it is easy to determine by that plain rule: "Whether ye eat or drink, or whatever ye do, do all to the glory of God."

— "A Farther Appeal"

The world never made any one happy; and it is certain it never will. But God will.

— July 5, 1783

You are no more at liberty to throw away your health than to throw away your life.

— July 28, 1775

I have often repented of judging too severely, but very seldom of being too merciful.

— Oct. 20, 1787

A string of opinions is no more Christian faith than a string of beads is Christian holiness.

Of all gossiping, religious gossiping is the worst: it adds hypocrisy to uncharitableness, and effectually does the work of the devil in the name of the Lord.

— June 20, 1772

There are two general ways wherein it pleases God to lead his children to perfection: doing and suffering. And let him take one or the other, we are assured his way is best.

— Feb. 17, 1774

The best of all is, God is with us.

— Last words of John Wesley

PART THREE

Faith and Life
(From Hymn Poems of Charles Weslay)
Charles Wesley Hymn Poems

ADORATION AND PRAISE

Being of beings, God of love,
   To thee our hearts we raise;
Thy all sustaining pow'r we prove,
   And gladly sing thy praise.

Thine, wholly thine, we pant to be;
   Our sacrifice receive;
Made, and preserved, and saved by thee,
   To thee ourselves we give.

Heav'nward our every wish aspires,
   For all thy mercy's store;
The sole return thy love requires,
   Is that we ask for more.

For more we ask; we open then
   Our hearts to embrace thy will;
Turn, and revive us, Lord, again
   With all thy fulness fill.

Come, Holy Ghost, the Saviour's love
   Shed in our hearts abroad;
So shall we ever live, and move,
   And be, with Christ in God.

THE TRINITY

Come, Father, Son, and Holy Ghost,
 One God in persons three;
Bring back the heav'nly blessing lost
 By all mankind and me.

Thy favor and thy nature too,
 To me, to all restore;
Forgive, and after God renew,
 And keep me evermore.

Eternal Sun of Righteousness,
 Display thy beams divine,
And cause the glories of thy face
 Upon my heart to shine.

Light, in thy light, O may I see,
 Thy grace and mercy prove;
Revived and cheered and blest by thee,
 The God of pard'ning love.

PRAISE TO CHRIST

O for a thousand tongues to sing
 My great Redeemer's praise,
The glories of my God and King,
 The triumphs of his grace!

My gracious Master and my God,
 Assist me to proclaim,
To spread thro' all the earth abroad
 The honors of thy name.

Jesus! the name that charms our fears,

That bids our sorrows cease,
'Tis music in the sinner's ears,
  'Tis life, and health, and peace.

He breaks the power of canceled sin,
  He sets the pris'ner free;
His blood can make the foulest clean;
  His blood availed for me.

He speaks; and listening to his voice,
  New life the dead receive;
The mournful, broken hearts rejoice;
  The humble poor believe.

Hear him, ye deaf; his praise, ye dumb,
  Your loosened tongues employ;
Ye blind, behold your Saviour come;
  And leap, ye lame, for joy.

———————

Ye servants of God, your Master proclaim,
And publish abroad his wonderful name;
The name all victorious, of Jesus extol;
His kingdom is glorious, and rules over all.

God ruleth on high, almighty to save;
And still he is nigh — his presence we have.
The great congregation his triumph shall sing,
Ascribing salvation to Jesus, our King.

Salvation to God, who sits on the throne!
Let all cry aloud and honor the Son.
The praises of Jesus the angels proclaim,
Fall down on their faces and worship the Lamb.

Then let us adore, and give him his right,

All glory and power, and wisdom and might,
All honor and blessing, with angels above,
And thanks never ceasing, for infinite love.

PRAISE AND RESPONSE

Come, let us who in Christ believe,
    Our common Saviour praise:
To him with joyful voices, give
    The glory of his grace.

He now stands knocking at the door
    Of ev'ry sinner's heart:
The worst need keep him out no more,
    Or force him to depart.

Thro' grace we harken to thy voice,
    Yield to be saved from sin;
In sure and certain hope rejoice,
    That thou wilt enter in.

Come quickly in, thou heav'nly Guest,
    Nor ever hence remove;
But sup with us, and let the feast
    Be everlasting love.

CHRIST'S SUFFERINGS AND DEATH

O Love divine, what hast thou done!
    Th' incarnate God hath died for me!
The Father's coeternal Son
    Bore all my sins upon the tree!
The Son of God for me hath died:
My Lord, my Love, is crucified.

Behold him, all ye that pass by,
The bleeding Prince of life and peace!
Come, sinners, see your Saviour die,
  And say, Was ever grief like his?
Come, feel with me his blood applied:
My Lord, my Love, is crucified.

Is crucified for me and you,
  To bring us rebels back to God:
Believe, believe the record true,
  Ye all are bought with Jesus' blood;
Pardon for all flows from his side:
My Lord, my Love, is crucified.

Then let us sit beneath his cross,
  And gladly catch the healing stream;
All things for him account but loss,
  And give up all our hearts to him;
Of nothing think or speak beside:
My Lord, my Love, is crucified.

MERCY

Depth of mercy! Can there be
Mercy still reserved for me?
Can my God his wrath forbear —
Me, the chief of sinners, spare?

I have long withstood his grace,
Long provoked him to his face,
Would not hearken to his calls,
Grieved him by a thousand falls.

Now incline me to repent;
Let me now my sins lament;

Now my foul revolt deplore,
Weep, believe, and sin no more.

There for me the Savior stands,
Holding forth his wounded hands;
God is love! I know, I feel,
Jesus weeps and loves me still.

REPENTANCE AND FAITH

Father, I stretch my hands to thee;
   No other help I know;
If thou withdraw thyself from me,
   Ah! whither shall I go?

What did thine only Son endure,
   Before I drew my breath!
What pain, what labor, to secure
   My soul from endless death!

O Jesus, could I this believe
   I now should feel thy pow'r,
And all my wants thou wouldst relieve,
   In this accepted hour.

Author of faith! to thee I lift
   My weary longing eyes:
O let me now receive that gift;
   My soul without it dies.

Surely thou canst not let me die,
   O speak, and I shall live;
And here will I unwearied lie,
   Till thou thy Spirit give.

How could my fainting soul rejoice,
  Could I but see thy face;
Now let me hear thy quickening voice,
  And taste thy pardoning grace.

PEACE

In him we have peace,
  In him we have power!
Preserved by his grace
  Throughout the dark hour,
In all our temptation
  He keeps us, to prove
His utmost salvation,
  His fulness of love.

Pronounce the glad word,
  And bid us be free!
Ah, hast thou not, Lord,
  A blessing for me?
The peace thou hast given,
  This moment impart,
And open thy heaven,
  O Love, in my heart.

Turn me, Lord, and turn me now,
  To thy yoke my spirit bow;
Grant me now the pearl to find
  Of a meek and quiet mind.

NEW BIRTH

O how happy are they,

Who the Saviour obey,
And have laid up their treasures above!
   Tongue can never express
   The sweet comfort and peace
Of a soul in its earliest love.

   That sweet comfort was mine,
   When the favor divine
I first found in the blood of the Lamb;
   When my heart first believed,
   What a joy I received,
What a heaven in Jesus' name!

   'Twas a heaven below
   My Redeemer to know,
And the angels could do nothing more,
   Than to fall at his feet,
   And the story repeat,
And the Lover of sinners adore.

   Jesus all the day long
   Was my joy and my song:
O that all his salvation might see!
   "He hath loved me," I cried,
   "He hath suffered and died,
To redeem a poor rebel like me."

   O the rapturous height
   Of that holy delight
Which I felt in the life-giving blood!
   Of my Saviour possessed,
   I was perfectly blest,
As if filled with the fullness of God.

WITNESS OF THE SPIRIT

How can a sinner know
   His sins on earth forgiven?
How can my gracious Saviour show
   My name inscribed in heaven?

What we have felt and seen
   With confidence we tell;
And publish to the sons of men
   The signs infallible.

We who in Christ believe
   That he for us hath died,
And all his unknown peace receive,
   And feel his blood applied.

We by his Spirit prove
   And know the things of God,
The things which freely of his love
   He hath on us bestowed.

HOLINESS

He wills that I should holy be,
   That holiness I long to feel;
That full divine conformity
   To all my Saviour's righteous will.

See, Lord, the travail of thy soul
   Accomplished in the change of mine;
And plunge me, ev'ry whit made whole,
   In all the depths of love divine.

On thee, O God, my soul is stayed,

And waits to prove thine utmost will;
The promise by thy mercy made,
  Thou canst, thou wilt, in me fulfill.

No more I stagger at thy pow'r,
  Or doubt thy truth, which cannot move;
Hasten the long expected hour,
  And bless me with thy perfect love.

O come and dwell in me, Spirit of pow'r within!
And bring the glorious liberty from sorrow, fear and sin.

The seed of sin's disease, Spirit of health, remove,
Spirit of finished holiness, Spirit of perfect love.

Hasten the joyful day which shall my sins consume,
When old things shall be done away, and all things new
  become.

I want the witness, Lord, that all I do is right,
According to thy will and word, well pleasing in thy sight.

I ask no higher state; indulge me but in this,
And soon or later then translate to my eternal bliss.

What is our calling's glorious hope,
  But inward holiness?
For this to Jesus I look up;
  I calmly wait for this.

I wait till he shall touch me clean,
  Shall life and pow'r impart,
Give me the faith that casts out sin,
  And purifies the heart.

This is the dear redeeming grace
    For ev'ry sinner free;
Surely it shall on me take place,
    The chief of sinners me.

When Jesus makes my heart his home,
    My sin shall all depart;
And, lo! he saith, "I quickly come,
    To fill and rule thy heart."

Be it according to thy word;
    Redeem me from all sin:
My heart would now receive thee, Lord;
    Come in, my Lord, come in!

O for a heart to praise my God,
    A heart from sin set free,
A heart that always feels thy blood
    So freely spilt for me!

A heart resigned, submissive, meek,
    My great Redeemer's throne;
Where only Christ is heard to speak,
    Where Jesus reigns alone;

A humble, lowly, contrite heart,
    Believing, true, and clean,
Which neither life nor death can part
    From him that dwells within;

A heart in every thought renewed
    And full of love divine;
Perfect, and right, and pure, and good,
    A copy, Lord, of thine!

Thy nature, gracious Lord, impart;
   Come quickly from above,
Write thy new name upon my heart,
   Thy new, best name of love.

Love divine all, loves excelling,
   Joy of heaven to earth come down:
Fix in us Thy humble dwelling:
   All Thy faithful mercies crown.
Jesus, Thou art all compassion,
   Pure unbounded love Thou art;
Visit us with Thy salvation;
   Enter every trembling heart.

Breathe, O breathe Thy loving Spirit
   Into every troubled breast!
Let us all in Thee inherit,
   Let us find that second rest.
Take away our bent to sinning;
   Alpha and Omega be;
End of faith, as its beginning,
   Set our hearts at liberty.

Come, almighty to deliver,
   Let us all Thy life receive;
Suddenly return, and never,
   Never more Thy temples leave:
Thee we would be always blessing,
   Serve Thee as Thy hosts above,
Pray and praise Thee without ceasing,
   Glory in Thy perfect love.

Finish then Thy new creation;
   Pure and spotless let us be;
Let us see Thy great salvation,

Perfectly restored in Thee:
Changed from glory into glory,
 Till in heaven we take our place,
Till we cast our crowns before Thee,
 Lost in wonder, love, and praise.

Jesus, thine all-victorious love shed in my heart abroad;
Then shall my feet no longer rove, rooted and fixed in God.

O that in me the sacred fire might now begin to glow;
Burn up the dross of base desire, and make the mountains
 flow!

O that it now from heav'n might fall, and all my sins
 consume!
Come, Holy Ghost, for thee I call; Spirit of burning, come.

Refining fire, go through my heart; illuminate my soul;
Scatter thy life through every part, and sanctify the whole.

My steadfast soul, from falling free, shall then no longer
 move,
While Christ is all the world to me, and all my heart is love.

Give me a new, a perfect heart,
 From doubt, and fear, and sorrow free;
The mind which was in Christ impart,
 And let my spirit cleave to thee.

O take this heart of stone away!
 Thy sway it doth not, cannot own;
In me no longer let it stay;
 O take away this heart of stone!

82

Cause me to walk in Christ my Way;
    And I thy statutes shall fulfill,
In every point thy law obey,
    And perfectly perform thy will.

O that I now, from sin released,
    Thy word may to the utmost prove!
Enter into the promised rest,
    The Canaan of thy perfect love.

Now let me gain perfection's height;
    Now let me into nothing fall,
Be less than nothing in thy sight,
    And feel that Christ is all in all.

Humble and teachable and mild,
O may I, as a little child,
    My lowly Master's steps pursue!
Be anger to my soul unknown;
Hate, envy, jealousy, be gone;
    In love create thou all things new.

Let earth no more my heart divide;
With Christ may I be crucified;
    To thee with my whole heart aspire:
Dead to the world and all its toys,
Its idle pomp, and fading joys,
    Be thou alone my one desire.

My will be swallowed up in thee;
Light in thy light still may I see,
    Beholding thee with open face,
Called the full pow'r of faith to prove,
Let all my hallowed heart be love,
    And all my spotless life be praise.

Come, Holy Ghost, all quick'ning fire,
My consecrated heart inspire,
   Sprinkled with the atoning blood:
Still to my soul thyself reveal;
Thy mighty working may I feel,
   And know that I am one with God.

CONSECRATION

Vilest of the sinful race, lo! I answer to Thy call;
Meanest vessel of Thy grace (grace divinely free for all),
Lo! I come to do Thy will, all Thy counsel to fulfil.

If so poor a worm as I may to Thy great glory live,
All my actions sanctify, all my words and thoughts receive;
Claim me for Thy service, claim all I have and all I am.

Take my soul and body's powers; take my memory, mind,
   and will;
All my goods, and all my hours; all I know, and all I feel;
All I think, or speak, or do; take my heart; but make it new.

Now, my God, Thine own I am, now I give Thee back Thine
   own;
Freedom, friends, and health, and fame, consecrate to Thee
   alone:
Thine I live, thrice happy I, happier still if Thine I die.

Father, Son, and Holy Ghost, one in Three, and Three in One.
As by the celestial host, let Thy will on earth be done:
Praise by all to Thee be given, glorious Lord of earth and
   heaven.
   (No sacred lyrist has ever more completely and concisely
embodied the sentiment of Paul's exhortation in Romans
12:1.)

CHRIST'S RESURRECTION AND HOLINESS

I know that my Redeemer lives, and ever prays for me;
A token of his love he gives, a pledge of liberty.

I find him lifting up my head; He brings salvation near;
His presence makes me free indeed, and he will soon appear.

He wills that I should holy be; what can withstand his will?
The counsel of his grace on me He surely shall fulfill.

Jesus, I hang upon thy word; I steadfastly believe
Thou wilt return, and claim me, Lord, and to thyself receive.

When God is mine, and I am his, of paradise possessed,
I taste unutterable bliss, and everlasting rest.

———————

I know that my Redeemer lives;
   He lives, who once was dead;
To me in grief he comfort gives;
   With peace he crowns my head,

He lives triumphant o'er the grave,
   At God's right hand on high,
My ransomed soul to keep and save,
   To bless and glorify.

He lives, that I may also live,
   And now his grace proclaim;
He lives, that I may honor give
   To his most holy Name.

Let strains of heav'nly music rise,
   While all their anthem sing

To Christ, my precious sacrifice,
And ever-living King.

THE LOVE OF CHRIST

"'Tis Love! 'tis Love! Thou diedst for me!
I hear thy whisper in my heart.
The morning breaks, the shadows flee;
Pure, universal love thou art:
To me, to all, thy mercies move;
Thy nature and thy Name is Love."

Jesus, Lover of my soul, let me to Thy bosom fly,
While the nearer waters roll, while the tempest still is high!
Hide me, O my Saviour, hide, till the storm of life be past;
Safe into the haven guide, O receive my soul at last!

Other refuge have I none, hangs my helpless soul on Thee:
Leave, ah! leave me not alone, still support and comfort me!
All my trust on Thee is stayed, all my help from Thee I bring,
Cover my defenseless head with the shadow of Thy wing.

Wilt Thou not regard my call? Wilt Thou not accept my
   prayer?
Lo! I sink, I faint, I fall — Lo, on Thee I cast my care:
Reach me out Thy gracious hand! While I of Thy strength
   receive,
Hoping against hope I stand, dying, and, behold, I live.

Thou, O Christ, art all I want; more than all in Thee I find:
Raise the fallen, cheer the faint, heal the sick, and lead the
   blind.

Just and holy is Thy name; I am all unrighteousness:
False, and full of sin, I am; Thou art full of truth and grace.

Plenteous grace with Thee is found, grace to cover all my sin:
Let the healing streams abound, make and keep me pure
within,
Thou of life the fountain art; freely let me take of Thee:
Spring Thou up within my heart, rise to all eternity.

GROWTH IN GRACE

Jesus, plant and root in me all the mind that was in thee;
    Settled peace I then shall find; Jesus is a quiet mind.
Anger I no more shall feel, always even, always still;
    Meekly on my God reclined; Jesus is a gentle mind.

I shall suffer and fulfill all my Father's gracious will;
    Be in all alike resigned; Jesus is a patient mind.
When 'tis deeply rooted here, perfect love shall cast out fear;
    Fear doth servile spirits bind; Jesus is a noble mind.

I shall nothing know beside Jesus, and him crucified;
    Perfectly to him be joined; Jesus is a loving mind.
I shall triumph evermore, gratefully my God adore;
    God so good, so true, so kind; Jesus is a thankful mind.

Lowly, lowly, meek and pure, I shall to the end endure;
    Be no more to sin inclined; Jesus is a constant mind.
I shall fully be restored to the image of my Lord,
    Witnessing to all mankind, Jesus is a perfect mind.

PEACE AND CONTENTMENT

Peace, doubting heart, my God's I am,
    Who formed me man forbids my fear;

The Lord hath called me by my name;
  The Lord protects, forever near:
His blood for me did once atone,
And still he loves and guards his own.

When passing thro' the wat'ry deep
  I ask in faith his promised aid,
The waves an awful distance keep,
  And shrink from my devoted head;
Fearless, their violence I dare,
They cannot harm, for God is there.

To him mine eyes of faith I turn,
  And thro' the fire pursue my way,
The fire forgets its pow'r to burn,
  The lambent flames around me play.
I own his pow'r, accept the sign,
And shout to prove the Saviour mine.

TRUST AND CONFIDENCE

Thou hidden Source of calm repose,
  Thou all-sufficient Love divine,
My help and refuge from my foes,
  Secure I am while thou art mine;
And lo! from sin and grief and shame,
I hide me, Jesus, in thy name.

Thy mighty name salvation is,
  And keeps my happy soul above:
Comfort it brings, and pow'r and peace
  And joy and everlasting love;
To me, with thy great name, are giv'n
Pardon and holiness and heav'n.

Jesus, my all in all thou art;
  My rest in toil, my ease in pain;
The healing of my broken heart;
  In war, my peace; in loss, my gain;
My smile beneath the tyrant's frown;
In shame, my glory and my crown.

In want, my plentiful supply;
  In weakness, my almighty pow'r;
In bonds, my perfect liberty;
  My light, in Satan's darkest hour;
In grief, my joy unspeakable;
  My life in death, my all in all.